CORPORATE TURNAROUND

CORPORATE TURNAROUND

A Practical Guide to Business Survival

PEDRO NUENO

Kogan Page Ltd, London
Nichols Publishing Company,
New Jersey

The masculine pronoun has been used throughout this book. This stems from a desire to avoid ugly and cumbersome language, and no discrimination, prejudice or bias is intended.

First published in 1992 by
Ediciones Deusto, SA
Barraincúa, 14
48009 Bilbao
Spain

Kogan Page Limited
120 Pentonville Road
London N1 9JN

Published in the United States of America by Nichols Publishing, PO Box 331, East Brunswick, New Jersey 08816.

British Library Cataloguing in Publication Data
A CIP record for this book is available from the British Library.
ISBN 0 7494 1131 7

Cataloging-in-Publication Data is available from the Library of Congress
ISBN 0-89397-398-X

Typeset by Saxon Graphics Ltd, Derby
Printed and bound in Great Britain by Clays Ltd, St Ives plc

Contents

Acknowledgements

Writing a book needs plenty of time for uninterrupted work. Those who have not been able to organize a sabbatical year, the privilege of academics and politicians, have no alternative but to use weekends and vacations. Hence, my first acknowledgement is to my wife Montse and my children Pedro, Christina and Carlos for their patience and understanding.

Second, I must thank the numerous employers, executives, union leaders, consultants, lawyers and officials with whom I have been able to work during turnaround processes or who have agreed to be interviewed on their experience in this field. The experiences they have conveyed to me have been invaluable and they deserve all the credit for this book.

Third, I would like to mention two colleagues to whom I owe a very large part of my knowledge in this field and with whom I have shared experiences and knowledge: Professor Fernando Serra of the IESE and Professor Wickham Skinner of the Harvard Business School.

Finally, I would like to express my gratitude to Montse Rivas, who has been my secretary for ten years and, in spite of this, still maintains excellent good humour, for her help in making this book a reality and in the preliminary research on which this book is based.

Due to the nature of the subject, any resemblance to reality is exactly what is intended but the appreciations and opinions included in the book are subject to the limitations of the author.

1

Introduction

In the early 1950s, the centre of one of the working-class areas of Barcelona hummed with the activity of a large textile mill, La España Industrial. At the call of sirens that were heard throughout the whole area, rivers of workers, still dressed in their overalls, flowed out from the factory into the Calle España Industrial, breaking up into smaller streams along adjacent streets such as Calle Masnou or the Carretera de Sants, as they made their way to their homes. From time to time, the flows changed direction to fill the factory at shift changes. Today, the factory is only a memory in aging minds, and where it once stood there is now a park. What at one time generated the wealth that enabled thousands of people to bring up their families today is a place where the grandchildren of those who worked there go and play. But parks do not create wealth.

A city without parks is an urban failure. But a city whose parks are victorious over industry, sooner or later, is an economic failure. At one time, people could walk to work; now, they have to travel for several hours in a car or by public transport. Perhaps some end up moving home to be nearer work and, little by little, entire districts of many cities become ghettos of misery where only the weak and old remain, unable to generate sufficient resources to survive and carry out even the barest minimum of maintenance to hold back the irreversible decline.

In Boston, Manchester and so many other industrial cities that moved in time to the wealth-creating to-and-fro of the shuttles, buildings similar to those that housed the looms of La España Industrial are now tombs to an extinct textile industry. The closed factories along the banks of rivers which in the past were their life blood are witnesses to industrial decline and failure. The Llobregat River in Catalonia is studded with many such cemeteries. The Merrimack in New Hampshire suffered the same fate. On the banks of the Merrimack was founded Manchester which, like its British namesake, lived off the textile industry, only to see it succumb with the passage of time to the competition of more modern factories located elsewhere, mostly in the south of the United States. And the same has happened in Flanders, in the Pas de Calais, and in so many other places.

In contrast, the decision was made to site many steel foundries and some chemical plants in coal-mining areas or in places with easy access to coalfields by sea or river. Europe and the United States still have many grandiose ghost foundries and huge rusting factories near to where coal is, was or could be easily retrieved. Sometimes, these iron giants—not brick this time—die sooner, broken up for scrap. But often their industrial death is hounded by lawsuits that will never end and which keep them chained and locked long after they are dead.

We spoke of closed mines and closed shipyards, now we can add to the list closed automobile plants and household appliance factories, with gloomy, interminable assembly lines, from which hang the rusting hooks that once carried along the various parts on their way to assembly. Competition, as one of the basic pillars of the market economy, is the cause of all this destruction. We do not mean that competition is bad, but is it necessary for competition to destroy so much wealth? The cost of replacing many of the ghosts we have just mentioned would be incalculable. The wastage of resources associated with industrial failure is enormous. The human suffering that accompanies unemployment, emigration, the breaking up of families, the frustration of expectations and dashed hopes cannot be quantified.

Some of these industrial ruins were a city's only source of industrial employment. Imagine what would happen to a prosperous city like Eindhoven in Holland if one day Philips and Daf—who have their corporate headquarters and main plants there and are the leading employers—were to close down or institute massive layoffs. Eindhoven has excellent educational facilities most of whose graduates take jobs in the city's main two industrial companies. There are good restaurants and hotels there that serve above all the floating population generated by the city's industries. There are bank branches, doctors, lawyers, tax advisers and translators who, like many small companies in Eindhoven, are suppliers to the two main companies or are suppliers to the people who work for them, providing them with food, clothing, furniture, car repairs, plumbing, glassware, building work, interior decorating, medicines, printed material.

When a large company that is a major source of jobs in a city falls ill, the entire city falls ill, and if the company dies, the city dies. The service society—the post-industrial society—is a sham. If one day, God forbid, Philips and Daf should fail, the bank branches, tax advisers, hotels, restaurants and taxi-drivers in Eindhoven will be unable to make up for the industrial wealth lost by producing services. That is why the inhabitants of Llodio in the Basque Country defend the town's steel mill, that is why the Asturians defend Ensidesa, that is why they defended the General Motors plant in Lynn, that is why the miners in Tharsis occupied the mine threatened with closure. When the company that provides the industrial jobs in a town closes, the services lose their basis for viability and gradually leave the town too.

We do not mean that only industrial companies are important; the failure of a service company is also a tragedy that we must try to avoid. However, the industrial company is the primary link in the wealth-creation chain and, if it breaks, its effects are felt furthest along the chain. Also, the paralyzation of industrial assets usually results in a greater wastage of resources as industrial companies are usually more intensive in plant and equipment. This is also the case in some service industries such as transport and telecommunications: the more highly developed a service, the more equipment it requires and the

9

more industrialized it becomes. Thus, for example, the air transport service is becoming increasingly equipment-intensive. When Eastern and Braniff failed, for example, the news reports showed us the sad spectacle of dozens of large planes parked immobile around their base airports, with their engines covered, awaiting the legal outcome of the disaster.

We all agree that the social good requires a fair distribution of wealth, and experience shows that the most effective means of distributing wealth is by creating more and destroying less. The countries that have achieved the greatest net increases in wealth are also those with a large middle class and a better standard of living. There is also a general consensus in the desire to continue to improve the quality of life with less effort, and most people can think of plenty of appealing things to do to occupy the hours of leisure that nobody would object to. Furthermore, both our solidarity and simple common sense enable us to see clearly that a balance between a rich Europe and a poor Africa, a rich North America and a poor Latin America or a few rich countries in Asia surrounded by other poor countries is not a stable one. In such circumstances, it is surprising that humanity continues to contemplate passively the frequent destruction of a country's industrial fabric. It is also surprising that governments do very little to avoid it. It is even more surprising that from time to time they even launch programmes to subsidize the closure of plants and industrial companies, using the wealth provided by some companies to finance the redundancies in others, and to convince employers to allow the destruction of their companies' industrial assets, thereby reducing competition and enabling others to survive.

The death of any company is often accompanied by a series of quantitative circumstances that are worth analysing a little. The fact that certain facilities have been completely or are almost completely depreciated does not mean that they do not have any value. Even when we say that an industrial plant is obsolete because of its size or technology, parts of this plant are usually still viable from both viewpoints. A certain percentage of workers who lose their jobs never find another one, particularly in societies such as Europe and North America which suffer chronically from high unemployment rates and will in all likelihood continue to suffer them due to immigration. In societies where the state protects those who have no resources, the real cost of making a person unemployed can be the present net value of paying that person an allowance for as long as he or she lives. Let us consider, for example, a country where theoretically a person can be made redundant with virtually no severance payment, such as the United States. Just in health aid for the needy, the state spends $110 billion each year on MEDICARE (1991) and $90 billion on MEDICAID (1991). We have not attempted to quantify the cost of the misery caused by unemployment but the sums spent by developed states in aid for retraining, housing and countless benefits are enormous and growing. When an industry is allowed to close, the cost is enormous, not only in the immediate impact of redundancy payments and waste but also in the delayed impact made up of aid that is difficult to quantify and a social cost that is impossible to express in numerical terms.

Unlike people, companies do not die suddenly. The heart attack does not have a counterpart in companies. Unlike with people, when companies fall ill, it is usually easier to diagnose the problem. In the field of corporate analysis, there is no such thing as an autopsy because when a company dies, the causes are usually clear long before the fatal event actually happens. It is obvious that we have no great love for companies. The various stakeholders (employers, managers, workers, creditors, customers, authorities) have different ways of loving companies but the fact is that all of them see companies fall ill, suffer, writhe in their dying throes and finally die, but fail to come to any agreement on how to avoid it. The death of a company is more like that of a person who has diabetes but does not follow a diet, who has liver problems but drinks, who suffers from chronic bronchitis but smokes, and although that person's health clearly deteriorates from day to day, he or she refuses to give up his or her health-destroying habits, with the passive tolerance of the person's immediate family, until the deterioration is irreversible.

The struggle to prevent deindustrialization is as old as industrialization itself. In his masterpiece *Scale and Scope*,* Alfred Chandler (1990) relates more about the effort made in the last century to save companies from a certain death. Since the Second World War, governments have resorted to a variety of formulas to prevent deindustrialization. On some occasions, nationalization has been used as the only way of covering the enormous costs of restoring an industry's health out of the state budget. On other occasions, restructuring plans have been used to obtain refinancing, financing under favourable conditions and subsidies for equipment, layoffs or the fulfilment of financial obligations. In recent years, there have even appeared 'turnaround specialists' who, either working on their own or as departments of expressly organized business groups, enter companies in serious difficulties and therefore in the process of foundering, to solve their problems and thus turn them around, with the aim of subsequently selling them at a profit.

Unfortunately, experience shows that revitalizing companies is not at all easy, and, in practical terms, it is virtually impossible that the state should succeed in the task. Even those who choose the noble profession of corporate lifesavers or turnarounders often swallow a lot of water in the process and many struggle back coughing on to the beach, with nothing in their hands and more than one broken nail, having found out for themselves the difficulty of reversing the momentum of a sinking company. The problem seems initially to follow such a textbook pattern that even the civil servants understand it and think they can solve it: companies A, B and C produce exactly the same products in an inefficient way (suboptimal size, obsolete technology, poor quality). The solution is to create a single holding company that coordinates them so that each specializes in a single product, investments are not duplicated, optimal sizes are attained, a more ordered supply enables better prices to be commanded,

---

* *Scale and Scope* is a probing analysis of the evolution of a series of industrial sectors in several countries by studying key variables in the configuration of competing industries and companies. It uses the historical analysis methodology.

and all these things together put the companies back on the road towards the black. The corporate lifesavers also explain what they consider typical patterns of reversible deterioration: the entrepreneur has only two daughters, one married to a doctor and the other is a nun; he has been milking the company—first a doctor's office for his son-in-law, then some apartments on the coast, later a little dabbling on the stock market; he has been progressively neglecting the company and sales have been allowed to drift; the all-absorbing character of the founder has never allowed a second layer of competent managers to be formed—it is simply a question of 'professional *management*'. It is not that easy: civil servants and private turnarounders usually find heavy opposition to conventional wisdom. Off-course companies do not respond docilely to turns of the wheel.

But, even so, it must be tried. It is worthwhile trying. Industry must be safeguarded. Declining companies must be revitalized. Turning around companies is good for the community, but it can also be good business. If those who hold the company's ownership do not wish or do not know how to continue, one must find another way to gain control. Today, there are many ways of doing this: management buyouts, privatizations, management contracts, etc. Our world increasingly accepts a liberal approach to economics and business and this attitude stimulates the creation of imaginative instruments that provide greater room for manoeuvre for those who assume such complex undertakings. Turning around companies can be a way of achieving levels of social recognition and wealth that would be beyond the reach of conventional entrepreneurial or professional career paths.

However, a dying company, like a fallen tree, can still provide food for many parasites. There are experts who are able to perform wonders in drawing out sap from virtually defunct companies, to the point of selling, when there is nothing else left, tax-saving capacity to another healthy company through the proper use of tax credits. This parasitic behaviour of companies raises a certain doubt as to the parasite's ethics which, even though no law is broken leads to a certain general unpopularity. We are not talking about this. When we defend the effort to revitalize companies, we are talking about the people who work with good intentions, who are trying to preserve the maximum number of jobs possible and to strictly fulfil all existing commitments with third parties. It is totally proper that those who undertake such projects should expect their efforts to be rewarded, but the reward should not come from appropriating what belongs to others; rather it should come from creating value, by managing to infuse value into something that was virtually worthless.

For the same reason, it seems reasonable that governments should take a favourable view of company turnarounds. It is the author's opinion that less government is better government, at least as far as companies are concerned. However, it is surprising to see sometimes how entire buildings are filled with civil servants working to apply a liberal government policy. These civil servants—ministers, secretaries of state, undersecretaries, general secretaries, general directors, etc—open and close events, grant interviews, make statements, write in the press and sometimes simply explain over and over again that the state should not interfere and that employers should not expect to receive state aid, backing their statements with first-class lectures in liberal economics. Perhaps it would be possible to reduce government deficits by getting rid of this type of civil servant and leaving the teaching of economics to the university lecturers. However, if ministers of industry, employment, technology or trade are absolutely necessary, it would be a good idea if they did something to prevent deindustrialization.

There are things that government can do to prevent the collapse of companies which do not imply either direct interventionism, which usurps from the employer his role as leader of the company, or a series of more or less discriminating subsidies. For example, sometimes employers complain that governments do not enforce international trade agreements. In Europe, for instance, there have been prolonged situations of dumping in the textile and steel industries, to name but two, while Brussels has done little to put an end to them. Sometimes, there still arise situations of unfair competition between public and privately-owned companies in developed countries. In

Spain, for example, private steel companies have expressed their dissatisfaction with the attitude taken by the publicly-owned company Ensidesa, which competes with them in some market segments in an unorthodox fashion and incurs heavy losses. The government's tolerance of very sick but sometimes highly politicized companies that do not carry their full cost load (tax, social security) allows these companies' disease to be spread to others.

The field of corporate turnaround has been little studied. In any process of this type, so many variables are involved that to find a global structure for formal analysis is unthinkable. We are therefore talking about something that is closer to an art than a profession. In the end, however, when a situation turns out well and one looks back on the process that has been followed, one discovers that basically one has only been correctly applying well-known management principles. Rarely is success attributable to the use of some sophisticated technique but rather to knowing how to lead a good team of managers and professionals. There are situations that tend to occur repeatedly in these processes, approaches that help to focus them better and suggestions that can help achieve a better final result. All this we will deal with in the following chapters.

METHODOLOGY

The approach is primarily practical and is based on analysing a sample of real-life turnarounds or attempted turnarounds. Our database consists of thirty turnaround situations that can be grouped into three categories: situations experienced personally by the author in his capacity as director or consultant of the company concerned; situations researched directly by the author, with extensive interviews of the process's key participants (some of these situations have been written up and published as a case study); and situations investigated by others authors and, generally, published as a case study. Many of these case studies are used as teaching material in the analysis of turnaround problems in various programmes of the IESE. All three categories have approximately the same number of observations. In the course of the book, partial descriptions of turnaround problems taken from this database will be used to illustrate some point. When the source is a published and available case study, bibliographic details will be provided.

No statistical processing of the data is performed as the purpose here is not to prove a certain hypothesis but to enrich executives' experience and to structure the reality of corporate turnaround in a manner that will help to explain it, understand it better and, above all, act. The author has not refrained from offering specific recommendations if he has seen for himself that such advice has given good results in several cases or, on the other hand, if certain other types of behaviour have not been very useful.

DIDACTIC CONCESSIONS

It is a fact that as English has become consolidated as an international business language, a series of terms appear in all fields of business management that are used untranslated in non-English-speaking countries. In this book, these terms are defined as they appear. To the reader who readily understands English, this may seem superfluous but there are many senior managers in Europe who do not speak English. After having been presented on innumerable occasions as a graduate of the University of Hardware (although perhaps for an engineer with ironware leanings, this might not seem to be an irreparable insult), of being asked about 'joint venture' when the proper term was 'venture capital' or 'just-team' instead of 'just-in-time', I have taken the liberty to provide a gloss on the original version of an activity as international as is 'turnaround', which, incidentally, is the term given to the process of refloating or significantly restructuring a company.

CONTENTS

Chapter 2 discusses in more depth the reasons why the managers of declining companies so often deceive themselves about the gradual deterioration that is taking place and allow the problems to grow to a size that requires unconventional and often traumatic solutions.

Chapters 3 and 4 discuss respectively two major categories of turnaround approaches: that of separating units and relocating them in other companies and that of revitalizing all of the company's units while preserving the unity of the whole. Although most turnaround processes usually contain parts of both approaches, they are sufficiently different and the circumstances surrounding them are so unique that it seems reasonable to discuss them separately.

Chapter 5 considers the time when there is no choice but to admit that the company needs a radical change of direction and, above all, investigation by people able to implement a turnaround process. The chapter discusses the profile of such people, the organization of the team that will work on the turnaround and its remuneration.

In turnaround processes, the people that manage the project are often not members of the organization in which the problem was created. The chemistry of the relationship between 'insiders' and 'outsiders' is the subject of Chapter 6. Chapter 7 analyses a series of types of people who are usually involved in turnaround processes or who sometimes at least try to become involved. These are intermediaries and specialists who can be very useful if they do their job properly.

Chapter 8 reviews recent literature on the subject of corporate turnaround and Chapter 9 includes a few final conclusions.

2

The capacity for self-deception

THE EXTENT OF THE PROBLEM

The company executive—and, even more so, the employer—has an extraordinary capacity for self-deception. When faced with difficult decisions or serious difficulties, this capacity for self-deception may increase. When things are going well and the good times cover a multitude of inefficiencies and structural problems, many people also deceive themselves by refusing to see what is lying hidden there under the carpet. Behind any process of corporate decline, there is an infinite string of deceptions. As a teacher who uses the case method, dozens of times I have asked groups of employers and managers analysing a case study on business decline, 'What mistakes did this company make?' In no time at all, the blackboard is filled with examples of miscalculation, indecision, omission, negligence, lack of foresight, waste and nepotism that have caused the process of erosion that has led the company to its present difficulties. Somebody always says, 'Inability to react.' And if I ask, 'But is it possible that they did not realize what was happening?', the overwhelming answer is 'No'. Everyone quickly comes to the logical conclusion: their actions were bad and the consequences were bad, but they did not want to see it—they deceived themselves.

CASE STUDY

At the end of 1985, when it was unmistakably clear that Spain was going to join the European Economic Community, most Spanish iron and steel manufacturers were able to continue to thank exports which were supported by what was euphemistically called a tax deduction, but which was, to a great extent, a subsidy paid on exports. As members of the EEC, Spain could not continue to subsidize an industry, but without subsidies, exports would be loss-making. The domestic market could absorb at the very most two-thirds of the national production but not at particularly favourable prices. In other words, either each company operated at 60 per cent of capacity, which is something of an industrial aberration in this sector, or one-third of the companies had to go. However, the employers either could not or would not appreciate the situation, and instead went to the Ministry of Industry to ask for alternatives to tax deduction. The officials at the Ministry did not dare say no and promised to study the situation. Four years later, several major companies in the sector had disappeared.

One of the first case studies I wrote at the beginning of my academic career was about a major European motor vehicle manufacturer. In the case study, which is available in the IESE's case study library,* there is a rather naive question I asked the company's president: 'Now that your company is profitable, don't you think that it's the right time to integrate with another group in your industry to achieve maximum economies of scale and technology?' This was obvious and, at that time, it would

---

* ENASA. Case study produced by IESE and included in its case study library under number P-298.

have been possible to do so in favourable conditions. The case study includes an elaborate answer explaining how the company could progress on its own. In the interview, the company's president explained that he received with a certain frequency visits from senior managers in other companies in the industry who would briefly enumerate their company's future development projects, including the models they would probably be launching and, above all, the likely new developments in key components (engines, for example). He admitted that these explanations were disguised offers for his company to join the industrial group the visiting executives worked for in order to avoid duplicating investments. However, perhaps he interpreted this as a sign of weakness on the part of his visitors. The company ended up going beyond the point of no return and, over the years, cost that European country's citizens a lot of money. It was finally integrated into another group but at the cost of losing a large part of its identity.

Is it possible that what was in the textbooks, what anyone slightly knowledgeable in industrial policy could predict, was not seen by that company's senior management team? It is difficult to believe that. A brief look at the world history of the motor vehicle industry reveals a slow but steady disappearance, since long before the time the case study was written, of those companies that were not large enough or sufficiently specialized. It is clear that the window period* in which it was still possible to do something was lost and then all the economies of scale which should have been achieved over the years, and which were lost, were paid for by the citizens of that country through their taxes.

---

* A window period is a period of time that all things have during which it is possible to do things and after which it is no longer possible. It is important to be able to calculate when the window will close.

Case Study

It was clear that Jumberca,* a Spanish textile machinery manufacturer, was not doing too well at the end of the 1970s. The company was involved in too many things at the same time: several production centres, a presence in very different markets (looms and knitting machines), world coverage of the market (it would not be possible to conceive of a company in the textile machinery industry in other way), an overlarge catalogue of different machines. And all this existed in extremely difficult economic circumstances: an urgent need to invest in capital equipment, and an oversized workforce with resulting abysmal productivity. At that time, the country was immersed in the process of transition towards democracy. The government had no industrial policy and the unions were primarily concerned with consolidating their own organizations, even though this would lead to the disappearance of the odd company as nobody was then aware of the unemployment problem that would appear a few years later. The company also had a terrible capital structure with heavy short-term borrowing at high interest rates, and it provided long-term financing for its sales with a high level of non-payers.

A summary of these problems, discussed in more detail in the case study, also raises the following questions:

- How is it possible for so many problems to be created at the same time, falling in the space of a few years from success to the danger of a major catastrophe?
- How is it possible that the management team could contemplate such a clear decline without taking corrective action?

---

* Jumberca. Case study produced by IESE and included in its case study library under numbers Jumberca, SA (A), no P-395, Jumberca, SA (B), no P-466, and Jumberca, SA (C), no P-490.

Perhaps the answer in this case could be found in the mistaken assignment of management responsibility to a person more qualified for product development, thus endangering two key areas: general management and product management. Miraculously, the company recovered its vitality and, ten years later, it was one of Spain's industrial successes, but it had been a very close shave.

A thought occurs: 'What must have been going on in the board meetings month after month?' No doubt, all of the directors, one of whom represented a major industrial bank which was partner of the company, were aware of the company's progressive deterioration and were able to diagnose where it was going wrong. So, why did they not do anything to change the company's direction? What did they say to each other to keep the deception going year after year? Did they resign themselves to thinking that the economic situation was going to change very shortly and that then everything would be put right? Did they accept losing the company providing that it did not cost them any money (thinking perhaps that they had already earned enough in the past)?

CASE STUDY

A Catalan textile entrepreneur made a major investment abroad. As is typical with some entrepreneurs, he decided to put one of his loyal employees in charge of the operation, but the person in question had never had any line responsibility nor did he have a suitable professional background. However, the business was well-designed and its approach was strategically advanced and relevant. Perhaps it was for this reason that the move did not go unnoticed by other employers in the industry or by observers of Spanish overseas investment. The entrepreneur himself was fairly heavily involved in launching the new subsidiary—things were done well, and there was no penny-pinching in the investment, which was set up right from the start in an attractive industrial park.

Little by little, the entrepreneur withdrew his personal involvement in the subsidiary, leaving it in the hands of his loyal employee. Immediately, the problems started: tyrannical treatment of the managers, irresponsible treatment of the personnel, irrational decision-taking, and the red ink started to flow. Everyone expected that the entrepreneur would react and replace his man there. One year later, things continued to get worse. The business problems were now compounded by the scandals associated with the employee's immoral conduct who often and without too much scruple mixed his disordered personal life with the company's business, charging to the company invoices covering his own high living and even riotous parties in the office. The flood of losses worried the Spanish overseas trade authorities as the company had to continually request authorization to increase its flow of funds to the foreign subsidiary to cover the losses. The authorities analysed the case in detail since this was taking place in the 1970s when capital flight was a widely practised and pursued activity. But the situation was clear—there were no capital flights, the subsidiary was losing money by the truckload. The authorities wondered how a company could lose so much.

The foreign subsidiary finally collapsed. However, before that happened, several horrified managers had left. How could the entrepreneur allow this man to squander so many millions of pesetas? Many had complained to the entrepreneur but the only answer they received from him were incoherent excuses protecting his man and indicating that things would change as soon as the start-up problems were sorted out.

In any industrial sector we care to analyse, between 1970 and 1991, we will see companies that have disappeared, having gone bankrupt and closed, or have been taken over or are still looking for a buyer, or are living on public funds, due to this irreversible disease: Alfa Romeo, Jaguar, Seat, Pegaso, British Leyland, Macosa, Corberó, CECSA, Torras Herrería y Construcciones, Banco Urquijo, Banco Catalán de Desarrollo, Lavis, Vanguard, Chrysler Europe, Isodel, Unidad Hermética, FECSA, Marconi, Explosivos Río Tinto, International Harvester, Korf Industries.

It was fairly clear that the demise of these companies would be more or less dramatic. It was also clear that these companies did not have the size, technology, balance-sheet structure, costs, or combination of these aspects, needed to survive in their respective industries but, somehow, their managements deceived themselves to avoid starting the hard and difficult processes that could have restored their health. All of them were at some time or other successful companies that had managed to differentiate themselves from others by finding a market niche and satisfying the needs of a group of customers, for example:

- Seat in the early 1960s;
- Isodel at the start of Spain's extraordinary electricicity growth;
- the model Banco Urquijo in the early 1960s;
- the dynamic industrial growth of the Banco Catalán de Desarrollo in the late 1960s;
- the incomparable international prestige of Jaguar.

Unfortunately, it would also not be difficult to write a long list of universally known companies that are today living in self-deception and sooner or later will have to face a harsh reality. In that list, we would find the odd large bank overburdened with unskilled personnel, little technological sophistication, minimal creativity and considerable product maturity. We would find insurance companies intractable from years of bureaucratic practice. We would find companies with cost structures that are just not viable in industrialized countries, and without the resources or time to change their situation in industries from textiles to toys, footwear to furniture, household articles and graphic arts.

REASONS FOR MAINTAINING THE DECEPTION

S elf-deception, while so clear, sometimes so collective and so lasting, has specific mechanisms that explain it, maintain it and perhaps justify it. The mechanisms of self-deception are sometimes so strong that they withstand the energy of high-calibre executives. The network of false arguments produces an enormous degree of internal resistance within the company and senior managers sometimes prefer not to face them for fear of an immediate upheaval that would be more shattering than a gentle decline. Probably, the ultimate self-deception is the hope of finding a different destiny before the final crunch.

CASE STUDIES

The controlling interest of Industrias Muntaner (I have disguised the name) had been held by the Banco Catalán de Desarrollo. By the early 1980s, Industrias Muntaner was managed by a managing director who reported to a board of 'bank men'. Among the directors, there was the head of another company owned by the bank, somebody who more or less occupied the position of 'manager of controlled companies' and a top manager in the bank group. In the early 1980s, the remains of the Banco Catalán de Desarrollo, together with the remains of the Banco de Madrid, were lumped together with what was left of the Banco Garriga Nogués and, it was said, all this was 'orbiting' around the Banesto bank, like asteroids, which are also remains, and which are also orbiting around out there.

The managing director of Industrias Muntaner was a hard-working man who knew his industry well, having spent all his working life in it. He was also a member of the family that had sold its share in the company to the industrial bank following a belief that many entrepreneurs had in the 1960s that things had gone so well that they could not continue like that indefinitely. After many years of making money, the best conclusion would be to sell the company to the bank at a good price. The sad fate of Spanish industrial banks during the decade 1975–85 showed that those intuitive entrepreneurs certainly knew their stuff. (History repeats itself and, after a few good years, the banks are rediscovering their industrial vocation— now's the time for entrepreneurs to use their intuition!)

As is usual, the managing director found the company rotten through. Little by little, he reorganized it. He replaced the members of his family that still held positions for which they were not qualified by more appropriate people. He cut down staffing levels. He invested in modern machinery. He strengthened the sales network. He improved the product. He transferred part of the plant to a new location so as to release urban land for sale. After years of untiring effort, Industrias Muntaner climbed back into the black. During that period, the managing director received subtle but insistent signs from his directors: 'Eliminate all of Industrias Muntaner's financial risk with our bank group; if you need discount lines, go to another bank; if you need to invest, go to the Banco de Crédito Industrial* or obtain credit from the machinery suppliers; we don't want any problems.' The directors never pretended that they understood the industry and gave a free rein to the managing director, although they constantly reminded him of this piece of financial policy. Most of the board meetings were spent talking about 'politics' in the bank's top management (of which there was no shortage) or in the country (of which, at that time, there was no shortage either).

---

* A state bank with which some employers thought that it was possible to renegotiate debts indefinitely.

Now back in the black and with such an unmotivating employer, the managing director thought that he could perhaps convince some of the members of his family to buy back their share from the bank. Perhaps he could reform a small family group that believed in him and were prepared to regain control of the company. His first tentative inquiries met with a positive response and he decided to undertake the project. The first step was to inform the bank. The board were not particularly pleased at the idea—to his surprise—but suggested he present an offer.

The managing director and his family group hired a consultant to calculate an objective valuation of the company. After delving into Industrias Muntaner to some depth, the consultant presented a study valuing the bank's share in the company between 50 and 70 million pesetas. The managing director agreed with the consultant's calculations but, putting a value on the incentive that heading a company that was partly his would have for him, at 50 years of age, and considering that with the additional motivation he would be able to ensure the most favourable conditions possible, he said that he and his family group would be prepared to go up to 100 million pesetas. The consultant said that, in his opinion, that was absurd and easily proved to him that 100 million in fixed-income securities would purchase, without any risk, much more than a company still loaded with excess personnel, still with a fairly mature product and yet only two years discretely in the black. But the managing director had more ambition in business than the consultant and he went to the bank with his proposal: 'First, I'll say 50 million, maybe they'll say 100 million and in the end we'll settle at 75—we'll split the difference.'

The board's answer admitted no negotiation.

'The book value of our share in this company is 300 million and we won't settle for anything less.'

'But there's no way of justifying those 300 million.'

'It doesn't matter, so long as you, the managing director, are at the helm, the company will function and we won't lose so why should we accept a write-down?'

'But,' he replied, becoming rather agitated, 'you've written off losses by the thousand, you must have provisions even to cover the cash, you've got more holes than a Gruyère cheese.'

The managing director went to see the bank's top management, where he found that the bank group's top management was like an Iberia bus on a rainy Friday, taking all the passengers from the 7.00 pm Friday Madrid–Barcelona shuttle to the terminal in one go: 150 people hanging onto their place and each prepared to take his neighbour's place from him if it turned out to be better. In an act of insanity, the managing director and his family offered 130 million pesetas but the board did not consider it appropriate and the top management was led by the lower levels.

The managing director soon understood that even if he offered 400 million, the transaction would not go through. There was too much top management in the bank group and too few companies to direct, control, supervise, assume responsibility for, etc. Monasteries are not usually burned down by their monks, and that monastery of managers would hardly be likely to offload companies that were the *raison d'être* of their jobs. The managing director understood that all that they expected from him was that he did not make waves. Years later, when the bank group's situation had degenerated to the point that many of the top managers had to leave their jobs, two of them admitted to the author that at that time there had been an implicit agreement to maintain an unstable equilibrium, jiggling with the bank's numbers—which was all the top dogs saw—to artificially prolong the life of a terminal patient. In such a situation, they were hardly likely to let go of companies that were not causing any problems and allowed them to justify their jobs.

A company had been formed after the Spanish Civil War, like so many others, by a financial partner and a technical partner. Its purpose was to make lamps. A little bit of capital to buy a few simple machines and small premises and the skill to obtain the raw material, at that time very hard to get, were the contributions made by the financial partner. The idea for the product, and the way of making it with unusual materials and very limited technical resources were the contributions made by the technical partner. The company flourished and became established as a leader in quality and design during the 1960s backed by a brandname that was well-known and sought-after both by the retailer and by the final consumer. The financial partner was successful in a number of industrial, commercial and financial business activities. The technical partner continued to run the industrial part of the lamp company.

When the economy entered a downturn in the 1970s, it became clear that the product was obsolescent although still with a respected brandname, the production equipment was outdated and the company was overstaffed. No corrective action was taken and, what was more, the crisis opened the doors to competing products manufactured in South-East Asian countries. In Spain, a number of semi-underground companies completed a picture of cut-throat competition.

The two founder partners had allowed their respective sons to enter the company in management posts so that, in a kind of attempt to project into the future the situation that had existed at the time of forming the company, one of the sons tended towards production and design and the other towards sales and finance. All four deceived each other mutually, concentrating on the fame of the brandname and playing down the lack of profitability. The company, which had done so well during the 1950s and 1960s, and even up to 1976, could revive at any time with renewed vigour and make its power felt. Some strange situation was keeping it temporarily dormant.

To speak to them about their obvious need to reduce personnel, the obsolescence of their factory, its deficient layout,* the insufficient cashflow for any truly effective restructuring of the business, that the competition would not go away and that sales did not multiply by magic, was like talking to a wall. None of the four were able to face a tough adjustment process and so they preferred to deceive themselves. And as there is always some blessed soul willing to give one a helping hand, finally, after talking over their problem with several possible consultants, they found a head hunter† who assured them that what they needed was a hard-willed, skilled manager who saw turning around the company as a step in his career, who would be prepared to complete their sons' managerial training, who would be able to put things in order and take difficult decisions. The two founder partners saw that they now had the solution to their problems and three months later they had their miracle-worker. Six months later, the miracle-worker had made his analysis: the situation was critical, extra capital had to be

---

* A company with vitality often changes its layout frequently. If one were to visit a 'live' operations centre on two occasions one year apart, one would be almost certain to find appreciable changes in the layout because distribution affects efficiency and continual improvements in the latter require changes in the former. In a declining operations centre, however, there are usually no changes in layout.
† Head hunter is the name given to those who specialize in seeking managers, normally taking them from other companies they are working in. They prefer to call their work 'executive search'. Their fees may be in excess of 25 per cent of the annual salary of the manager they place. Some highly security-conscious executives maintain cordial relations with two or three head hunters, just in case. Some head hunters are truly excellent professionals in a difficult art.

pumped in urgently or the whole thing could blow up at any time. Almost one year later, the two founder partners found themselves sliding further downhill, having to throw more money into a bottomless pit with the uncertainty of not knowing what would happen next.

At the end of 1989, the Spanish Ministry of Industry started the process of privatizing the special steel manufacturer ACENOR,* of which it had initially gained control as a result of its indebtedness with public sector institutions. A series of changes in the Ministry put the process in the hands of unskilled civil servants. The company was progressively deteriorating due basically to excessive debt and an oversized workforce, and as each month went by in 1990 the company's situation became more and more desperate. Two major industrial groups were prepared to buy ACENOR. One of them brought as partner the world's leading special steel manufacturer, Daido Steel Ltd, from Japan. In one way or another, the companies that were negotiating to buy ACENOR expected that the government would provide the necessary funds to settle part of the company's enormous debts and to reduce the workforce by about 1,000 people. Without this, it would never be possible to get a return from the investments that would have to be made in the company. However, communication problems between the two candidate buyers and the officials in the Ministry led to negotiations being dropped. Finally, the Ministry decided to create a state-owned holding company with ACENOR and another ailing nationalized company.

---

* The story of ACENOR can be analysed in depth in the series of case studies ACENOR (A) P-750, ACENOR (B) P-751, and ACENOR (C) P-752, and ACENOR (D) P-765, in the IESE's case study library.

By then, the government had two feasibility plans for ACENOR, one drawn up by one of the aspiring purchasers with the help of McKinsey, and the other drawn up by the other aspiring purchaser with the help of Daido Steel Ltd. The manager of the holding company then had the bright idea of asking for another feasibility plan, this time from the Boston Consulting Group. When the third plan arrived, in mid-1991, the situation in ACENOR was untenable. The company's liquidity problems were so severe that there was a danger that it would not even be able to pay its payroll, having already delayed payment of other, less vital items. During this period, practically nothing had been done in the company to combat this situation.

We could continue with hundreds more examples of situations at the bottom of which is the desire not to face reality. No doubt this attitude is not exclusive to the business world. It is probably also the attitude of the bad student, of those whose marriage is on the rocks, of the person who drinks or smokes too much, and of those in many other such situations. It is probably one more indication of man's fallibility.

There is a proverb in Catalan that says *qui dia pasa, any empeny,** which exemplifies the hope that effort in the short term will solve the long term. When dealing with employers or managers involved in such self-deception, on more than one occasion we come across a hyperactive person, continually immersed in mega meetings, travelling untiringly, but carefully avoiding facing the real problem: the company has no future unless something drastically different is done. The need to be at one and the same time active and avoiding reality can even lead the employer or manager to take up a training programme, as if it were possible to find magic solutions in the classroom. The reader can be sure that out of every 100 employers or managers participating in a training course, two or three are there hiding

---

* He who passes a day, pushes a year.

from reality, seeking a way to fill their minds and postpone facing what should be their professional priority. On the other hand, instead of rushing around ourselves we can get someone else to do it for us, and commission a five-star consultancy to draw up a feasibility plan. That way, we fill the company with top-notch professionals, the agenda with working meetings full of overhead projectors, and we can say 'we're working on it'.

THE LACK OF ENTREPRENEURSHIP

One of the common initial causes of business decline is the lack of an entrepreneur, the absence of anyone who really sees the company as his and demands that his managers get results. A lack of entrepreneurship may come about for many reasons: apathy abandonment or incompetence. Apathy usually affects overpowering entrepreneurs who were able to create a company and make it grow to a certain point but are then unable to establish systems to attract good quality managers or organize a mix between ownership and board of directors that is able to continue imposing discipline, hard work and performance. In such cases, the company ages with its founder and sometimes more or less dies with him.

Abandonment is more typical of those who think they have done enough with their company and are not interested in carrying on, especially if carrying on means a more complicated management. This is usually the case with multinational companies in developing countries. They invest there in very favourable conditions, with an enormous tariff protection, a monopoly situation, and grants for installing plant and importing equipment; for a few years, they enjoy this preferential situation and earn fabulous profits which they repatriate as dividends or royalties, or more or less disguised as transfer prices for components. However, there comes a time once the market has grown when it is impossible to maintain this situation: local competition appears and pressures to cut back on privileges and allow other multinationals and importers to enter the market are inevitable. Then, those who enjoyed the enormous advantages may no longer feel motivated to work in the tougher environment and pull out. In Spain, for example, the case of Isodel* is one instance of how one company amassed riches from the electrification market in Spain during the 1960s and 1970s and then abandoned the subsidiary Isodel, accepting the loss of capital. A similar decision taken by the Dutch multinational Akzo with regard to La Seda de Barcelona is another example of abandonment.

When a company has been abandoned, it is sometimes not all that obvious to outsiders. The position may well not be cut and dried, and there may be managers for and against in the parent company. As a result no major investments are approved, but it is not made explicit that the parent company is no longer interested in its subsidiary and, of course, the ailing subsidiary is not provided with the best managers under orders to put it back on track. As things get worse, the parent company management may feel tempted to transfer shares to the workers, cede them to some parasite—there is always one somewhere—or any other solution that allows them to escape from the collapse. Depending on the industry, it may be that the final collapse will not happen until several years after the *de facto* abandonment as companies always carry with them a certain degree of inertia.

Incompetence is more typical of state-controlled companies, although it may also appear in family businesses when succession in management is necessarily dependent on surname. In the private sector, it is rare that a company with annual sales exceeding $1 billion would accept anyone as president who could not show a successful record in similar-sized business units. In the public sector, it may happen that a person with no previous experience in management is appointed chief executive of a major company. In most cases, such people will not be total incompetents, and it is possible that they have done a good job as civil servants or politicians. But being president of a large company requires years of experience which can only be

---

* A detailed analysis of this situation can be found in the case study Isodel, SA P-615, available in the IESE's case study library.

acquired by starting from the bottom, in small business units, and gradually working up.

State-owned companies are usually the main tenure of the trade unions, which is a little strange considering that it is these companies that usually have the most comfortable working conditions and operate with the least uncertainty. On the other hand, in healthier, growing companies, union presence is usually low. In state-owned companies, there is often a certain amount of comradeship between management and unions. This comradeship is not beneficial as it detracts from the company's purpose, which is to create wealth and not act as a showcase for union achievements, and is a formula that leads inexorably to decline.

Many managers of state-owned companies have no difficulties in justifying themselves. The state-run company pays poorly. A public manager may earn 10 per cent of what a private manager in his industry earns and up to 1 per cent of what a competing owner-employer accumulates. The salaries of top managers in state-owned companies are closer to those of civil servants than to the professional manager market and this is a mistake. Probably the best solution would be, not to raise the salaries of these public managers but to privatize the state-owned companies and let the new owners decide.

SYMPTOMS OF CORPORATE DECLINE

There are many symptoms that an employer or senior manager can perceive to diagnose the worsening condition of his company. Table 2.1 shows some of them, which we will discuss in more detail below.

If we analyse the years of decline of companies whose owners—private or public—were not prepared to rectify the situation, we see a parallel flow of valuable people leaving the sinking ship. The French companies that were nationalized by Mitterrand lost valuable managers. The large Italian corporations, whose leaders seemed to have been intimidated by the tough recession of the 1970s, lost valuable management personnel until those same leaders recovered their energy (Agnelli) or other leaders took over the torch (Schimberni, De Benedetti). In

Spain, Seat lost valuable people until it was bought by Volkswagen, Pegaso suffered a continual drain of managers from the
mid-1980s and Torras Hostench lost many people until the KIO
Group came in. Citibank lost many professionals before its crisis
became apparent in 1990. The loss of human resources is one of
the clearest signs of deterioration and is, at the same time, an
extraordinary impoverishment that accelerates this deterioration as it leaves the company without any ability to react.

Table 2.1 *Symptoms of corporate deterioration*

- Loss of key managers
- Loss of profitability
- Loss of market share
- Deterioration of liability structure
- Sales increasingly based on price
- Resistance in the financial community
- Reticence among suppliers
- Increasing labour hostility
- Increase in non-payers
- Loss of productivity

The loss of profitability is another unmistakable sign for the
management that the company is in a process of decline. In
order to remain competitive in a certain activity, a company
must reinvest each year sufficient funds to train its personnel,
update its product, modernize its facilities and finance its
growth—and do all these things without affecting its capital
structure. This is what we could call maintaining the
entrepreneurial thrust. All this requires a minimum cash flow.*
When the cash flow is insufficient for maintaining the
entreprencurial thrust, it is like when a sick person has a

---

* Cash flow here means the self-generated funds that are available in the
company, and is basically profit after tax plus depreciation. In cases of
restructuring, there may be subsidies or aid—taxable or not—whose net value
can be added to these available funds.

progressive anaemia. It is true that it is possible to put off investments or borrow, but these actions often worsen the cash flow shortage, starting a spiral of decay.

The loss of market share is another symptom of weakening that can pass unnoticed more easily, especially in times of economic boom. In Spain, for example, during the years following membership of the European Economic Community (1986–1990), the economy grew at a very strong rate. In such an environment, some companies experienced high growth rates and operated with production facilities at full capacity. However, the market grew even quicker and imports gained market share. Once they have gained a position in the Spanish market, it is not easy to dislodge these foreign competitors and in the years of lower growth following the boom, the companies that lost market share suffered the consequences of their smaller relative size in the form of lower returns, lower use of capacity, loss of attractive market niches, greater demand for quality and differentiation, etc.

Corporate decline is usually correlated with a process of deterioration of the liability structure. Each economic activity usually requires a certain capital structure. In steel-making, chemicals, petrochemicals, textiles, basic foods, one cannot conceive of a capital structure which includes a lot of debt. In these industries, 50 or 60 per cent shareholders' equity is a reasonable liability structure that will enable the company to ride over market oscillations. Obviously, the capital structure depends to a certain extent on the type of loans offered on the capital market. In Japan, where interest rates are low and long-term credit is a reality, in the industries mentioned above it would be possible to have a capital structure with only 30 per cent shareholders' equity while still maintaining a healthy situation. However, in Europe, and particularly in Spain where the capital market is still relatively undeveloped, a company's capital structure should be less leveraged. A succession of years with decreasing or negative results, perhaps aided by ill-conceived investments, and all this accompanied by an unwillingness to increase share capital, may lead to a liability structure with 10 per cent or less shareholders' equity. If interest rates shoot up, they finally gobble up the diminishing industrial margin. Companies like ACENOR, Ensidesa, Altos Hornos de Vizcaya and La Seda de Barcelona at the end of 1990 are good examples of this unfortunate situation.

When price starts to become the main point on which getting orders hinges, it indicates that it is the only thing that is differentiating the company. That means that its customers are probably sending it orders for the most standard items and demanding the best conditions. As it will not always be the case that the company in question is the industry's most efficient competitor, more often than not it is margin that is being sacrificed.

The financial community usually has a good nose for detecting company decay. This does not mean that they immediately stop lending money to the company. Generally, as the company's debts increase, they seek more guarantees, try to finance more controllable assets (imports, exports, specific sales), limit financing to shorter terms and, above all, increase the interest rates. The company's manoeuvrability in the financial market becomes more restricted and this also limits any effort to redress the situation.

Suppliers are usually more aware than the banks of their customers' state of health and react in a similar way, demanding cash payment for their deliveries, charging higher prices and diverting away long-term interest in the sick customer, thus effectively cutting him off from information flows and integration in product development.

A situation of company decay without any attempt by the management to correct it usually creates a greater inflexibility among the workers. A good personnel management is usually able to convince a workers' committee to accept sacrifices that clearly improve the company's ability to compete. However, staff reductions that are merely cutting off successive slices of the company in the process of its gradual destruction are generally strongly resisted by the workers' committee and the trade unions. In situations of sustained decay, the committee may become entrenched in absurd stances in which what would be obvious to anyone, such as the need to improve productivity or the desirability of making better use of a complex and expensive facility, is rejected out of hand. Unless there is a reorganization plan that clearly answers all doubts, the committee will not modify its unbending stance.

As the saying goes, when it rains it pours, and it is generally true that companies that have been losing competitiveness for several years usually have higher levels of bad debts than their healthy counterparts. It may be that their sales representatives, anxious to meet their quotas, are not very careful in selecting customers; it may be that the customers know that the company is unlikely to threaten to stop selling to them; it may be that the sales administration department is not on its toes. It will probably be a combination of all these things and others, but the fact is that the slow payers in an industry tend to accumulate in its weaker companies.

When there are large productivity gaps between companies in the same industry, such gaps have usually been widening over a period of several years, because some companies have improved their productivity very quickly while others have done so more slowly. This can be seen in Table 2.2. Considering that it is always possible to gain a certain amount of information on competitors' productivity, it is surprising to see that some companies allow their productivity to drift increasingly further from that of their competitors. If we talk of a difference of only one car per worker per year between two companies that produce five and six cars respectively, at a cost of £15,000 per worker, the company that only manages to manufacture five is being penalized by £500 per car compared with the company that manages to make six, due to its lower productivity. This cost disadvantage may lead to a certain gradual decapitalization, lower investment in products and distribution and even to a neglect of training. At the same time, it may help the more efficient competitor to become the pricing leader in the market.

From Table 2.1 we have analysed a list of ten symptoms—the most important—that help diagnose decline in a company. It is possible that these symptoms are interrelated to a certain extent. In general, it is usually possible to obtain for a series of companies specific measures for the variables whose deterioration we have called symptomatic of decline. It must therefore be possible to compare the values of these variables for one's own company with those of other companies in the industry and thus determine the precise rate of decline. It is usually observed that healthier companies continually compare their own performance with that of their main competitors and keep all the employees informed of the differences found, while sick companies have little information on their competitors or prefer to ignore it.

Table 2.2 *Productivity in motor vehicle production adjusted for levels of vertical integration, use of capacity and differences in personnel costs*

| | *Vehicles per employee by year* | | |
Year	GM, Ford, Chrysler*	Nissan	Toyota
1965	4.7	4.3	6.9
1970	4.6	8.8	10.9
1975	5.3	9.0	13.7
1979	5.5	11.1	15.0
1983	5.7**	11.0	12.7

* Average figures for GM, Ford and Chrysler.
** The 1983 figures for Ford and GM (not Chrysler) assume the same vertical integration levels as in 1979.

Source: Cusumano (1985).

THE DEATH OF A COMPANY

One renowned Harvard Business School professor once told us in class: 'I don't know if you'll be able to manage a company reasonably well, but I'm almost sure that you will never completely kill one.' Companies have such a great vitality, their ability to withstand is so high, their tolerance of things being done badly is so great that it is almost impossible to kill a company quickly. The only way to kill a company is by doing it little by little. If you shoot it in the heart, it survives bleeding for a long time. A company must be poisoned or malnourished, all of its parts must be pushed into a process of irreversible decay. So long as any one of its parts remains alive, the company can be regenerated from this single part. If companies were more fragile, then perhaps the people running them would take the processes of decline more seriously. This natural strength aids and abets the deception process.

However, some people are entitled to include in their list of achievements that they have killed a company. These people wield great power in the company, they grab hold of the helm and do not let go, even though tons of water wash aboard every time the ship crashes into a trough. They are the type who think that only they possess the truth and therefore they are most unwilling to listen. They are the type who do not readily admit to having made a mistake and therefore insist in following the direction they have chosen. They are the type who are unable to create a powerful management team or, if they have such a team, they are unable to work synergistically with it. They are highly subjective people, visionaries, and even have leadership ability, but they have little practical skills and are little prone to analysis. This provides the necessary conditions for keeping the process of deterioration going for long enough to ensure the company's permanent demise.

CONCLUSION

T he ability possessed by owner-employers and top man-agers to deceive themselves as to the state of decline their companies have reached is extraordinary. The situation is all the more serious when the deception is collective; many managers, directors and analysts avoid saying explicitly, 'This isn't going to get us anywhere.' Instead, they resort to creative accounting, to image campaigns, to wringing the last drop of money from any sellable asset, in order to be able to carry on without facing reality. Individual interests, incompetence in the specific turnaround task, lack of interest on the part of the owners, political priorities, these are motivations that may become intertwined to prolong the deception and, with it, the steady deterioration of the company.

However, it is not difficult to detect and even measure this deterioration well before what we could call the 'point of no return'. All it requires is to compare a series of ratios and other aspects with those of competing companies, and to include all the levels of the company in this comparison. If a manager or employer were to draw a matrix with the ten variables we have analysed in this chapter, for example, include in it scores for their own company and their main competitors, and then reproduce this information for the last five years, they would clearly see in which direction their company was headed. If the trend reveals a state of deterioration, there is no need to wait any longer; one must act immediately or quickly find someone else who can.

3

Save the whole or salvage the parts?

Obviously, these are not the same things. A company is a very complex entity made up of shareholders, workers, managers, customers and suppliers, to mention only the human groups most directly affected by an activity consisting of producing a certain value added by manufacturing goods or providing services. Almost always, a turnaround requires a little surgery, as there are usually some parts of the company that are in such an advanced state of deterioration that it is unthinkable to put resources into revitalizing them. However, if the surgery is very extensive, then perhaps we should not call the process turning around. It would be like taking an injured loved one to the emergency department of a hospital and receiving a few hours later the following advice from the surgeon: 'You've got nothing to worry about, all his organs function perfectly; of course, they have been transplanted into different recipients, since the patient was in such a bad state that his organs together would not have been able to support each other.' There are cases in which it is possible to save the day: there are no layoffs, the shareholders do not lose their assets and the suppliers are paid their bills, but it cannot be said that the company has been turned around. This does not mean that it is not better to save the pieces than to lose everything, but the two things are not the same.

CASE STUDY

A capital equipment manufacturer had started to pile up losses. The company's main shareholder was a bank and, after many years of it being known that 'company X belongs to bank Y', the only option the bank had was to lend money to the company to keep it going. The bank owned quite a few more companies and to allow one of its companies to go bankrupt was an alternative it probably found unacceptable. The company had few customers because it served a highly concentrated market and the industry was in a downturn worldwide. To make things worse, the company utilized obsolete technology and after years of operating with a small order book, its productivity had sunk to minimum levels and its personnel spent part of their time with nothing to do. The bank owners had put 'bank-minded' managers at the head of the company, who had set about cutting all cuttable expenses and accounting perfectly for everything that was happening in the company, but they had no idea how the company could be taken out of its predicament.

Faced with this situation, the bank contacted an expert in failing companies who was also well-acquainted with the workings of the government, state-owned companies and trade unions. At about that time, a state-owned company had to make a large order for equipment of the type that could be manufactured by the ailing company. Given the high technological level of the products to be purchased, they could only be bought from abroad and two suppliers appeared as favourites: one in Germany and one in France. The expert in question managed to come to an agreement with both the French and the German suppliers so that part of the order could be manufactured in Spain, using the technology of the company that received the order. He was also able to take advantage of a propitious moment on the capital market to carry out a series of ingenious capital expansions that brought in a large amount of money into the company. With the money received, he paid off a large part of the debt accumulated with the bank.

When the state-owned company made its order, thanks to the agreements made beforehand with the foreign suppliers, the manager was able get one of them to take on most of the company's personnel and some of the industrial assets. Other assets, not directly related with the main line of business, were sold to other companies and the personnel were transferred with the business. These moves freed up a large plot of land in a large city, which suddenly turned into a negotiable asset—something that had remained hidden in the company's accounts, undervalued and, perhaps, even half-forgotten. Using the value of the land, the manager borrowed again and purchased a major holding in a well-known real estate company.

Thus, over a period of about three years, he managed to save almost all the jobs and transfer them from a failing company to a multinational; pay back to the largest creditor most of its debts; place a realizable value on a significant, semi-hidden asset; give an attractive business content (real estate) to the company, which had been emptied of its assets (industrial, but obsolete); and, thanks to the increased worth of the land, preserve a large part of the value of the investment made by the company's shareholders.

This is a case of major surgery in which the different organs are saved but transplanted to different places. This type of procedure perhaps cannot be called turning around but no doubt it is just as difficult. It requires realizing that the company could never sort out its future by optimizing its operations in its own line of business. It then requires being able to make an abstraction, break down the company into a thousand different forms and analyse how the parts can be moved to maximize the value of the whole. If a large order is won, it can be handed over with the personnel required to manufacture it. If the land can be separated from the workers that are on top of it, its value can be increased. If there is a side business, perhaps its market share can be auctioned among the main competitors. In general, this type of work requires a close-knit team, audacity, creativity, considerable negotiating skills and knowledge of accounting and financial engineering.

Sometimes, this type of manager comes under attack in the press, and even in the cinema, especially when they themselves have obtained an attractive return from the process of cutting up and transplanting the company. It is very difficult to establish what could be a suitable remuneration for a major operation of this type. It is a fact that, a priori, the party in difficulties is almost always prepared to offer a generous reward to anyone able to solve the crisis, particularly if it is in kind, such as shares of doubtful future value, or assets that can be freed if things go well or else be swallowed up by the catastrophe, such as commissions on the sale of the excised pieces, etc. It is also a fact, once the job has been done, that someone had to do it, that blood has been spilled, or that things could have been done better another way, and a lot of people will give their opinion on what has happened. To those not faced with the anguished helplessness of a downward spiral, the remuneration of the managers of this type of turnaround almost always, a posteriori, seems to be excessive. The fact of the matter is that, both in Spain and in the rest of Europe and the United States, those who have specialized in such cut up and transplant turnarounds may have their customers but it can hardly be said that they are liked.

In Belgium, independent distributors are well protected by law. If a manufacturer decides to change distributor or carry out the distribution itself, it must pay quite a large compensation to the distributor which has lost this business. Because of this, some manufacturers find themselves trapped because their distributors are inefficient but it would be too expensive to change distributor or distribution system.

CASE STUDY

Antwerp Engineering Distribution (AED) was an old Belgian company specializing in the distribution of technology-intensive products for industrial plants. Over the years, the range of products distributed by AED had grown extraordinarily and, in 1990, together with truly advanced items such as sophisticated sensors and analysis devices based on innovative technologies, the company also distributed standardized devices and equipment that had by now become commodity products. This development was in part the result of the passing of time. The manufacturers they distributed for continually added new items to AED's catalogue. However, the lack of a sales strategy led to insufficient specialization. The sales organization was too expensive to distribute commodity products and insufficiently trained to distribute very specific products. The extensive range carried meant very high stock levels with innumerable reference numbers and spare parts and a very low rotation. Administration was complex. In general, AED had too much staff and a very expensive organization.

The company's owners were members of a family with interests in several large companies in Belgium. For them, AED was not a very important company and was administered, rather than managed, by a man very close to the family. The company had not been asked to provide dividends for many years and the family had even approved a capital expansion recently to maintain the good capital structure that AED had always had. However, at a meeting of the board of directors held at the end of 1989, some members of the family made it very clear that something had to be done with the company soon and it was decided that one of them, Paul, the president of another successful company in the family group, would propose a solution by early 1990.

After studying the situation, Paul presented the conclusions of his analysis to the members of AED's board of directors. One almost obvious solution was to change AED's management. The new management should carry out a reorganization which would require dropping certain product lines, probably look for others, and significantly reduce the number of employees. This would take time and quite a lot of money and, even then, it was not clear whether the desired final result would be achieved. The solution which consisted of selling the company was probably not practical as a sale would give the distributed manufacturers the option to cancel their contracts without compensation and it was highly likely that most of them would seize the opportunity. There was another alternative that Paul had explored with a consultant friend of his who was very knowledgeable on food product distribution in Europe. This alternative consisted of negotiating their freedom with the manufacturers for whom they distributed. The manufacturers would be allowed to organize their distribution however they wished, either directly themselves or through another independent distributor. In exchange for this freedom AED would serve them for as long as they should require, that is they would facilitate the transition without leaving the market unattended, and the manufacturers could take on those items of the balance sheet associated with their accounts (customers, suppliers, inventory) and the people that most directly managed their products.

The board decided in favour of this solution of liquidating the various distribution agreements. By mid-1990, skillfully negotiated by Paul, 70 per cent of the personnel and a similar percentage of the inventory, customers and suppliers had been allocated. The approximately 30 per cent of the company that remained basically consisted of the distribution of more standardized products with less skilled personnel but, by now, it was a much smaller business unit. Paul negotiated with a group of managers, persuading them to take over the company in exchange for generously capitalizing it at the time of transferring ownership. These managers also undertook to manage the transition period.

In this case too, all the parts of the company remained alive, thus avoiding conflicts, risks and possible costs for the owning family. The lack of vocation in the family to reorganize AED without breaking it up did not cause unemployment, loss of market or non-payment of invoices. If, due to negligence or incompetence, AED had deteriorated to the point of declaring a suspension of payments or bankruptcy, then what would have naturally happened would probably have been the same. The various manufacturers distributed by AED would have stepped in to reorganize their distribution and some executives would have become small, self-employed distributors, but, in the process of deterioration and the ensuing crisis, there would have been losses, redundancies and non-payments.

TRANSPLANT TECHNIQUES

One prerequisite is the family's permission. The surgeon can't constantly be popping out of the operating theatre to discuss the details of the operation with the patient's family or to ask permission to cut a bit more off from this organ that seems to be affected or from that organ that does not seem to have a clear chance of recovery but which may require a second operation if he does not take more off now. The parties (owners, boards of directors, states) that delegate a turnaround of the type we are studying to such a person must give full powers for acting, with the risks that that involves.

An interesting aspect is the dismembering of the sick company. A textbook dismembering, which is probably that which would be followed by a recently graduated MBA* or a wholesale consultancy, would no doubt be based on product-market criteria or what is sometimes called business units. Thus, for example, a large chemical company may be cut up into a petrochemical part, a fine chemical part, a transport part, and a consumer product part (made with materials obtained in petrochemicals or fine chemicals). The industrial assets, the current assets, the personnel, even the managers, would then be distributed among these four units† and one would thus obtain four coherent, different, separated and separable units, to the point that each could be sold to different buyers.

A leader in this type of disaggregate turnaround may possibly carry out an 'opportunity-driven breakdown', guided more by what could interest different buyers. Thus, it is possible that he could form different packages consisting of land, some brandnames, a distribution network and a group of separate industrial facilities with certain liabilities, so that by merging them with another company, they could give capital gains and, therefore, greater future amortisations and lower tax payments, etc. In this type of breakdown, the manager is thinking how he can optimally place all the parts and not so much in building coherent units. He does not look inside companies but outside them, to the community of possible buyers. In order to do this job well, one needs to have a good understanding of the environment, have a lot of contacts, create innumerable scenarios, no matter how absurd they may appear, and explore the alternatives with appropriate experts and intermediaries.

A breakdown turnaround manager is an expert in valuation. The price of things depends on what someone is prepared to pay for them and this in turn may depend on a suitable market being created in which to sell them.

---

* MBA, or Master of Business Administration, is the academic title usually given to professional training in business management. A good MBA programme will require between 3,000 and 4,000 hours of postgraduate work and even a certain amount of job experience.
† Left to their own devices, experts could identify 20 or 30 business units in companies like Repsol or CEPSA, or perhaps 50 in ICI or British Petroleum. However, such large numbers are too unwieldy.

Case Study

A terminally ill company had a lift manufacturing division which was in a terrible state but which had a reasonable amount of plant and an interesting volume of maintenance work. At a time when the industry leaders perceived the need to eliminate companies from the industry and increase their share in the maintenance market, a skilled transplant manager was able to practically auction the ailing division, getting two large companies in the industry to bid competitively against each other.

What for one may not be worth anything—or may even have a negative value—for another may be worth something. The trick is to make things worth something for another person and find a way, better if it is indirectly, of letting him know about it.

Case Study

A paint company had a product range for the marine industry. The drop in shipbuilding meant that this product line started to lose money. The same thing happened with other companies supplying the marine segment of the market. Our company was able to make a major paint company that was not involved in the shipbuilding industry interested in buying its business. A competitor of the potential buyer, which in normal circumstances would not have been in the least bit interested in buying our company's down-at-heel marine paint business, perceived as a great danger the entry of a new, strong competitor in a market that was already very tight. In such conditions, our company was able to get a price for its ailing business that was not related to its state of health but to the strategic opportunity of providing a new competitor a means of entry (or preventing it, in this case) into the industry.

The break-up of a company may be facilitated by spinning off pieces of it to form independent companies. The task is to identify activities that could viably exist on their own and managers prepared to become entrepreneurs. Producing a spin-off may enable the structure to be lightened, as a number of managers and workers will leave with the new unit that has been created. If the company is on the point of finally foundering, those who go with the spin-off may view themselves as being taken off to safety in a life-raft. For the new company to be viable, it will need part of the parent company's working capital. In some cases, the new company may gain access to financing in its own right via loans or venture capital. One breakdown manager found the way to persuade a group of managers to take on parts of the company as independent companies. To motivate them to do so, he granted them bonuses which enabled them to capitalize themselves, on the understanding that they would use the bonuses to invest in the new companies. Thus, the operations with future prospects, the managers with most potential and the best workers were separated off from the rest. Some time later, what remained of the company suspended payments and was subsequently liquidated. As in any turnaround process, the ethics of the decisions must be carefully analysed but the spin-off, if properly used, can be a very valuable instrument.* In recent years, a variant of the spin-off has become very popular. We are referring to the 'management buyout'.† The liberalization of the capital market has enabled leveraged purchases of industrial operations by management teams to proliferate. Who better than the managers who ran the operation to make it grow once free of the deadweight of other

---

* The author has analysed in certain depth the spin-off technique as a tool for working in companies in difficulties in Chapter 4 of the book *New Patterns of Work*, edited by David Clutterbuck.
† In the management buyout, the managers buy all or part of a company and pay the owners the agreed price. Generally, the managers borrow or obtain the money for the purchase and they back the loan with the value of what they are buying (leveraged buyout). Chapter 5 of the book *Instrumentos financieros al servicio de la empresa* by G Pregel, R Suñol and P Nueno provides a detailed discussion of the concept of management buyout.

loss-making appendages. By selling off units through management buyouts, some companies have been able to recover funds by selling something to the only buyers able to truly value its potential.

The management of a spun-off unit may be assigned to a third party (individual or company) by means of an agreement that can range from a lease, in which this third party will pay to manage and then return the unit in some agreed fashion, to the management contract, in which the third party will be paid to manage the company. It may appeal to some companies to control certain production facilities which, otherwise, could end up on the market at any price in a disordered fashion. In such circumstances, a company may be prepared to finance the purchases and sales of the unit it manages under a lease, freeing the lessor from this responsibility and lightening his load.

The breakdown and transplant manager is able to use simultaneously all these techniques and more which have not been included here. This not only requires creativity but also a considerable power of conviction and, above all, tenacity to solve the thousand and one problems that arise when trying to turn these approaches into reality. Table 3.1 lists the techniques we have discussed in the preceding pages.

Table 3.1 *Some turnaround techniques through company breakdown*

- Separation into business units
- Opportunity-driven breakdown
- Formulation of different valuations of different groups of components of the company
- Spin-offs
- Management buyouts
- Leasing
- Management contract

CONCLUSION

A nyone who watches the ashes of a corporate crisis will see how the parts of the company which has disappeared naturally reappear in different places. The desire of some managers and employees to survive together with their entrepreneurial ability or the opportunistic vision of some customers, suppliers or competitors will cause the fragments of the dead company to be grafted on to other places. The collapse in the 1970s of a series of pioneering Spanish companies in various sectors of the electronics industry—Enclavamientos y Señales, Telesincro, Lavis, Vanguard, Cecsa, etc.—gave birth to a multitude of new companies to exploit a better defined market segment or to carry out more rationally a certain activity.

Reflecting on this transplant surgery, it occurs that perhaps, if done in time, it may provide a solution for many companies at the end of their road. However, there probably comes a time in the life—or perhaps we should say in the death—of a company after which it is no longer possible to apply this methodology: the fragments are too far gone and death is inevitable. But after death, the fragments will try, in spite of everything, to resuscitate themselves. In spite of the unpopularity of this type of solution for sick companies, employers, directors and senior managers should not rule out the alternative of using it as soon as they diagnose a difficult future. For the same reason that we all try to find out who are the good surgeons and how we can contact them, company managers too should find out who those few true professionals in the art of corporate transplant are and how to contact them.

4

Corporate turnaround by component regeneration

There is another way of revitalizing companies which, for many, is the most difficult and consists of something like turning the whole company to move in another direction, so that a series of destructive trends are reversed and what was producing increasing losses again becomes a generator of wealth. To achieve this with virtually the same workers, supervisors and managers, with the same factories, offices or shops, with the same products, seems to be little short of a miracle. However, Emilio Martínez Chueca in Jumberca, Bartolomé Parera in Hispano Química, John Harvey-Jones in ICI, Jan Carlzon in SAS, Luis Magaña in FECSA, Mario Schimberni in Montedison, Alfredo Sáez in Banca Catalana, Francisco Rubiralta in the CELSA Group, Joaquín Zueras in Colomer Munmany, Barry Gibbons in Burger King, and many others, have shown that it is possible and, in some of these cases, have shown that it is possible to do it more than once. The risk of quoting names is that, with the passing of time, people who achieved a resounding success at a certain historic moment may also fail in another. We are talking about a very difficult problem—turning around companies—and it must be expected that those who accept this challenge frequently, sometimes will not achieve their purpose. It must also be accepted that in some cases a turnaround may not be consolidated indefinitely. The company is saved but it is left weak and it may not be possible to salvage it in the next downturn. So, when I quote specific cases, the reader should not think, 'But that's the guy who screwed it up last month.' Let us give him the credit he deserved at that time. Physicians who treat seriously ill patients necessarily have a high proportion of cases whom, unfortunately, they are unable to restore to health, but that does not mean that we appreciate their work any less.

CASE STUDIES

At the end of the 1970s, the company Colomer Munmany, one of world's leading tanning companies, was in serious difficulties. Colomer Munmany, with its main industrial core in Vic, near Barcelona, and subsidiaries in Spain and a large number of foreign countries, was suffering from the problems generated by the economic recession that was affecting Europe and, more than most, Spain. This general situation was compounded by a fashion trend that was not particularly favourable to leather; the normal sequelae of an expansion process that was still continuing; the consequences of a family ownership with a strong entrepreneurial leadership concentrated in a single person but with marked shortcomings in important management areas; and the occasional incorrectly taken key decision, such as, in this industry, the purchase of raw material.

The company had asked for help from an agency that had been recently created by the Autonomous Government of Catalonia known as CARIC, whose initials—translated—stand for Catalonian Industrial Restructuring Aid Commission. This agency had been provided with relatively limited funds considering the immensity of the problem its name theoretically made it responsible for. CARIC decided to use these funds to guarantee loans to companies in difficulties providing that, in the opinion of the experts that comprised the agency's board, the company had a feasibility plan which enabled one to reasonably expect that it could be turned around and the loans could be repaid. The aim was thus to operate in a middle band between those companies that were not so ill that the financial community refused to attend to their plans and those companies that were so beyond hope that, for anyone who believed in the market economy, the best thing was to let them die and thus strengthen the business fabric as a whole. Among other organizations, CARIC's council also included representatives from business schools. Who was better qualified for carrying out the difficult task of determining whether the patient was terminal, semi-terminal or only mildly ill? And who was better qualified to determine the merits of a feasibility plan?

The author, who represented the IESE on CARIC's board, lived the Colomer Munmany experience at very close hand. If the company did not receive an additional loan of between 200 and 250 million pesetas, something terrible could happen to it and it could even be forced to declare a suspension of payments. Even with a guarantee from CARIC (with the backing of the Generalitat of Catalonia), it was by no means sure that the banks would want to be involved, having already put a lot of money into Colomer Munmany. At a meeting held with the representatives of the banks in the meeting room of the Department of Industry, the joint efforts of the civil servants and the academic enabled a compromise to be reached to the effect that the banks would wait, the guarantee would be authorized and new loans would be granted for the sum guaranteed. However, all this was subordinated to the implementation of a feasibility plan which had been developed. One of the key elements was the identity of the person who was going to add business professionalism to the entrepreneurial leadership of Andrés Colomer. The 'professional' executive in this case was Joaquín Zueras, who had been recruited to Colomer Munmany because of the crisis and who had been in difficult business situations before and had managed them successfully. Joaquín would have to bring in a few more people to strengthen specific management functions specified in the feasibility plan, realize a few assets not linked with the main business and drastically alter purchasing and stock management, among other things.

Between them, Joaquín Zueras and Andrés Colomer turned the company around in a couple of years and it was one of the CARIC's success stories. However, far be it from the author to extol CARIC's virtues. Its approach was fairly theoretical and most salvage plans promoted from the public sector are theoretical plans. However, sometimes these plans work when they support the right person.

In 1980, the company Unidad Hermética, located in Sabadell near Barcelona and which several years later would be purchased by Electrolux, was faced with a problem of excess supply and low productivity. Unidad Hermética's product—refrigerator compressors—had become a commodity as its technology became commonplace worldwide. Manufacturers from all over the world, including developing countries, offered compressors. The world demand had flattened out. It had almost 2,000 workers at a time of maximum union belligerence which was particularly aggressive in the metal industry and in companies that more or less headed their various industries, a description that was applicable to Unidad Hermética. Its facilities could not be adapted to manufacture products other than compressors. It was still living with the inertia of the 1960s and early 1970s of strong growth and high returns, and it had an expensive loan structure and a professionalization process that was only semi-implemented. In short, the company would have needed at least two or three years more with a strong market to complete smoothly all the adjustments it needed to be efficient and competitive.

The management considered several alternatives, from an abrupt downscaling to the size of the demand which could have meant making redundant one-third of the total workforce, to an urgent diversification, trying to manufacture some product that was industrially compatible with compressors. Finally, the management team, headed by the president Mr Forrellad and the general manager Mr Oliver, decided for a 'flight forward' approach. The plan consisted of improving productivity and costs through a significant increase in production. This production increase would be achieved by making maximum use of the potential of the existing workforce; thus, 10 per cent of the workforce performing indirect labour tasks (warehouse, transport, administration) were transferred to direct labour.

The solution was fraught with hazard in that it presupposed that the productivity improvements would reduce costs so much that it would be possible to place the entire production in profitable terms even though it would be necessary to reduce the price. This 'flight forward' required a certain amount of investment in equipment—not too much as, in general terms, it was possible to make better use of the existing plant—and above all in current assets (raw materials, products in process, finished products). It would also be necessary to urgently train the workers who would be transferred from indirect tasks to direct tasks. Also, a sales programme would have to be drawn up to place the new production level without driving market prices down below profitable levels.

The management team informed the workers' committee of the decision that had been taken but the committee did not initially accept the idea of shortening operation times, much less the transfer from indirect jobs to direct jobs. Unidad Hermética had to withstand a bitter strike that lasted for slightly more than one month but the management team refused to budge from its position. Finally, the strike ended, the plan was successfully implemented and the company was able to climb back out of its downturn.

During the same period, a North American competitor of Unidad Hermética's,* faced with a similar situation, opted for a much more daring reorganization alternative. The company separated its different ranges of compressors and virtually built new factories for each range. These factories were specifically 'focused' on each range's manufacturing needs. That is, layout, equipment, labour and organizational system had all been custom designed for the specifications, quality requirements and mass production of each product range. In this case too, the turnaround was successful.

The York Insurance Company,† a subsidiary of a powerful business group, faced a problem of progressive deterioration of its income statements during the early 1980s. Its premium revenues were virtually stalled at about £6.5 million. With 140 salaried employees, a high number of commission agents with high commissions, an outdated product range, an enormous internal bureaucracy caused by compartmentalization and excessive division of labour, predominance of personnel with low skill levels, and chronic underuse of data processing equipment, it is not surprising that the company was in decline: £345,000 in losses in 1981, £610,000 million in 1982, £655,000 in 1983. In premiums per employee, the

---

* See the series of HBS case studies Copeland (A), (B), (C) and (D).
† Disguised name. See the York Insurance Company case study, produced by IESE and included in its library list under number P- 520.

company held 68th place out of the top 100 in 1981 and 81st place in 1983. Its solvency margin, an important ratio in the industry, fell from 37th place in 1981 to 76th place in 1983. These trends were a cause of increasing disheartedness and frustration among the company's best agents but the management bureaucracy was unaware of the growing destructive inertia.

In service companies, the inertias can be stronger than in industrial companies because the business is people-intensive. The process depends entirely on people, many of them professionals, and on the coordination between them. Improving skill levels, reorganizing the professionals' work and changing internal communication circuits is slower and more time-consuming than cutting staff levels in a factory and getting the same production from the people and machines remaining.

A new management team sponsored by the parent company concluded that the only way to survive was to drastically improve productivity. In order to achieve this, they could promote a higher-growth product— such as multi-risk insurance—the level of computeriz- ation could be increased, and the professionals' tasks could be 'lengthened', thus avoiding the excessive atomization of work, the coordination difficulties this caused and the backlog of files in process. All these actions would require a certain amount of training. The improvements in operations, which would be noted particularly in the quality and shorter comeback time, would without doubt raise the agents' morale. However, the situation had gone so far that it would be difficult to increase sales quickly to a level that would put the company back in the black.

Fortunately for this company, the considerable fragmentation of the insurance sector in Spain meant that there were a lot of companies in difficulties. Once York had straightened out its operations system, the company's parent company purchased another fairly

complementary company in order to be able to mater-
ialize the improvements in effectiveness by combining
portfolios.

TURNAROUND APPROACHES

When turning around a company, work has to be
undertaken on a very broad front. For each individual
case, a turnaround must be designed that fits the
specific circumstance surrounding the problem. Turning
around companies by regenerating the various layers of the
corporate tissue is thus a very complex task, and perhaps less
spectacular than the transplant system as well as more difficult
to study. However, it is possible to classify most turnaround
operations into a series of different patterns. The cases described
above illustrate some of these patterns. In the following pages,
we will study them in greater depth.

Improving specific variables

Although it is not the most usual, it may happen that the
company's deterioration is the result of changes in a few independent and selectively treatable variables. Thus, for example, one
company's ills may be due to excess borrowing and an oversized
workforce. Table 4.1 gives a summarized operating account for one
particular loss-making industrial company. After modelling the
key ratios from the more aggressive competitors in the industry,
the company's management team reached the conclusion that
they should bill about £125,000 per person (instead of the present
£100,000) and that interest expenses should not exceed 4 per cent
of annual sales. The lower billing per employee was due solely to
low productivity, while the higher interest expenses were due to
an over-leveraged capital structure for the industry, forcing the
company to resort to an excessive degree to high interest short-
term loans and bank discounting.

Other aspects, such as technology, sales productivity, product quality, administrative management, etc., were in line with
the best companies in the industry.

Table 4.1 *Summarized operating account of an industrial company*

	£m	%
Sales	50.0	100
Purchases of materials, components, energy and supplies	27.5	55
Personnel*	7.5	15
Sales expenses	4.0	8
Administrative expenses	2.0	4
Financial expenses**	3.5	7
Other general expenses	4.5	9
Depreciation	2.5	5
Profit before tax	−1.5	−3
Cash flow	1.0	2

  * 500 employees at an annual cost of £15,000 each.
** Resulting from the permanent use of an average of £12.5 million in bank discounting lines at 17 per cent and £8.5 million in short-term loans at an average rate of 16 per cent.

A simple calculation shows that a capital injection of £9 million would put the company on the same level as its best competitors from the financial cost viewpoint. However, a staff reduction of 100 employees would put the billing per employee on a par with the industry leaders. Both measures together would represent an injection of £3 million in the operating account, which would now show a profit of £1.5 million and a cash flow of £4 million.

The problem to be raised then was the possibility—and, if applicable, the profitability—of implementing these two measures. As regards capitalization, there were a number of possible actions: customer collections could be brought forward from 90 days to 60 or 30 days; the loans could be refinanced at a lower interest rate; the short-term loans could be turned into long-term loans, with a mortgage guarantee and a lower interest rate; a partner could be attracted to increase the capital stock, etc. The workforce problem would mean studying the possibility of measures such as voluntary redundancy plans, early retirements, temporary layoffs or a combination of all of them. The art of managing a turnaround operation is to reduce the cost of restructuring to a minimum, to do it quickly and to avoid disruptions due to conflicts.

Table 4.2 *Types of measures to be taken in a turnaround plan*

Measures to achieve improvements in worker productivity
- Reduce operation cycle times
- Reduce workforce
- Transfer indirect labour to direct labour
- Increase output
- Redesign tasks/working groups

Measures to achieve improvements in liquidity
- Obtain subsidies and public grants
- Dispose of assets not required for operations
- Reduce stocks
- Reduce collection time
- Extend payment time
- Capitalize debts
- Renegotiate loan terms
- Increase capital stock

Measures to improve the working atmosphere
- Policy of keeping the workers' committee/trade unions informed
- Ongoing negotiations
- Split up general problems of large groups into specific problems of small groups

Measures to improve plant productivity
- Concentrate production in less plants/equipment
- Increase shifts
- Reduce set-up times
- Coordination/specialization/production swaps

Measures to improve the sales price
- Selective price increases in segments (by product, by geographical area) where there is less risk of a competitive reaction
- Downwards integration
- Via investment in processing/distribution
- Via joint ventures with processors/distributors

Measures to improve quality and service
- Increase awareness of middle management
- Rationalize product range
- Redesign product

Depending on the case, the combinations of variables to be readjusted may be virtually infinite. Table 4.2 shows some types of action that can be taken to improve certain variables. Which of these actions are chosen will depend on careful analysis, and implementation must be negotiated, firm and prompt to be effective.

Fitting the size to the demand

This is the approach that usually comes to mind immediately when corporate turnaround is discussed. The more mature sectors of the economy tend to be characterized by a permanent excess of capacity. Even though companies are continually closing, the capacity installed is usually greater than that which can be absorbed by a static or slowly growing demand. On the one hand, high cost competitors see cost reduction through increased productivity as their only option and the only way they see to increase productivity is by getting more output from their plants and workforces. On the other hand, the non-existence of technological barriers attracts investors from recently industrialized countries who, with low costs and sometimes very modern facilities, can compete advantageously. Hence, particularly in Europe and the United States, textile mills, steel mills, shipyards, electronic product factories, factories making any type of components, small household appliances, tools, toys, footwear and a long list of other products are never able to break free of the imbalance between market supply and demand. Consequently, a common approach is to adjust the production capacity to a market segment allowing differentiation and in which one can compete in less marginal conditions.

Adjustment to a smaller size has one problem: a large size helps hide problems better and enables the company to cope with inefficiencies better. When the size is reduced, new, previously unapparent problems appear.

The owners of a plastic products factory expanded their factory during a period of high growth. They built an enormous factory able to supply the entire national market and part of the

European market and they did it all on debt. The boom encouraged other manufacturers to do the same. Everyone must have thought that the demand would continue to grow indefinitely at the same high rate. It soon became clear that the excess capacity installed would never be used efficiently. To cap it all, the product began to be imported from Brazil and Korea.

After a few years of losses, the conclusion was reached that by concentrating on a very high quality market segment, the company would be able to achieve an appreciable differentiation and compete profitably. To attain this differentiation, the company only required one-third of the workforce and half of the plant. Sales would fall to slightly over half. Thus, the company would be smaller but very profitable. But what about the loans? A smaller company would never generate sufficient profits to meet the interest payments and return the loans outstanding. Where will it find the money for the redundancy payments? Finally, it resorted to a suspension of payments as a means of spreading its financial commitments over a longer period of time and perhaps reduce them. Little by little, it managed to whittle down its workforce and get back into the black. However, even so, the weight of the debt, even after restructuring, proved to be unbearable.

Adjustment is a technique that can be used particularly when there are no significant obstacles to workforce reductions. In Europe, in general, it is not feasible to use this technique. Many companies resort to employing a percentage of their workforce under temporary contracts and to subcontracting part of their production as mechanisms to allow them to make certain adjustments when necessary. Spanish legislation allows the use of 'employment regulation procedures'* as a means of making temporary adjustments to the workforce. Adjustment of financial commitments is only possible through the use of the suspension of payments, or as some employers put it, by means of a 'negotiated suspension of payments', which basically

---

* This scheme allows part of the workforce to be laid off for a certain period of time with the cost being shared between the government and the company. It must be approved by the employment authorities.

consists of convincing creditors that they either renegotiate the conditions of the debt while everyone is still friends or be forced to renegotiate after a suspension of payments in less favourable conditions.

The flight forward

This expression describes all those processes in which the company's size is increased, instead of reduced, in the attempt to take it out of its crisis. In the face of the difficulties in reducing the workforce, the management tries to offset this by increasing volume; if a substantially higher output can be obtained from the same workforce, the unit cost is reduced and therefore the price can be lowered. A lower price may then generate a greater demand to absorb the increased production.

Another way is to obtain control of sources of supply or major customers, or both, in an attempt to control as much as possible of the value added chain. In many industries, the profitability of the various phases of the business along the value added chain may vary according to the prevailing situation: today, raw materials earn more money, tomorrow it will be industrial products, the day after tomorrow consumer products, and at another time it will be the retailers. By controlling the various levels, it is possible to ensure a balanced return over time. There is always some phase that can achieve a greater degree of differentiation, and integrating the phases extends this differentiation to a certain extent to the rest.

Figure 4.1 shows the impact on profits of such a project based on transferring indirect workers to direct production tasks. In the baseline scenario, 1,000 units are sold at £1.5 million each, using 150 direct employees and 50 indirect employees. In scenario 1, it is assumed that the 50 indirect employees are transferred to direct labour tasks even though their output is only half that of the others due to their lack of training. This enables 1,166 units to be produced and they are placed on the market at a 5 per cent price reduction. Even so, the profit is increased by almost 90 per cent. Scenarios 2 and 3 show the enormous potential of converting indirect personnel into direct personnel under other, more favourable hypotheses.

Baseline scenario	**£**
Sales: 1,000 units at £1,500 each	1,500,000
Materials: £300/unit	300,000
Direct personnel: 150 employees at £3,000	450,000
Indirect personnel: 50 employees at £3,000	£150,000
Utilities £60/unit	60,000
Total production expenses	960,000
Gross margin	540,000
Financial expenses: 4% of sales	60,000
Sales expenses: 10% of sales	150,000
Fixed expenses	240,000
Total overheads	450,000
Profit before tax	90,000

	SCEN. 1 £	SCEN. 2 £	SCEN. 3 £
SALES (1,166 units at £1,425)	1,661,000	1,749,000*	1,999,000**
Materials: £300/unit	351,000	351,000	399,000
Direct personnel: (200 employees at £3,000)	600,000	600,000	600,000
Indirect personnel:	—	—	
Utilities: 60/unit	69,000	69,000	81,000
Total production expenses	1,020,000	1,020,000	1,080,000
Gross margin	641,000	729,000	919,000
Financial expenses: 4% of sales	66,000	70,000	80,000
Sales expenses: 10% of sales	166,000	175,000	200,000
Fixed expenses	240,000	240,000	240,000
Total overheads	472,000	485,000	520,000
Profit before tax	169,000	244,000	399,000

Scenario 1: The 50 indirect workers are transferred to direct labour tasks, although their output is 50% of a direct worker, which enables 166 more units to be produced. The price of all the units is reduced by 5% in order to be able to sell the 166 additional units.

Scenario 2: This would be the case if all 1,166 units could be sold without reducing the price.

Scenario 3: This would be the case if, in addition, the transferred indirect workers' output was the same as that of the direct workers, which would enable 333 units more to be produced than in the baseline case.

* 1,166 units at £1,500.　　　　** 1,333 units at £1,500.

Figure 4.1 *Turnaround by transferring indirect workers to direct labour: summarized operating accounts*

Redesigning the production system—focused production and flexible production

In some cases, the company's decline is the result of having built an excessive degree of complexity into the production process: over-wide product range; large variety of processes; wide range of different machines; large orders, small orders and urgent orders all issued at the same time; highly automated phases beside manual processes; high vertical integration with phases that are difficult to match; etc. The complexity leads to the proliferation of coordination instruments and the implementation of elaborate control systems that end up needing a lot of people to run them. The result is usually increasing costs and decreasing efficiency.

Back in the 1960s Wickham Skinner* recommended his concept of 'focused production' to solve this type of problem. As Figure 4.2 shows, the first step is to classify production into homogeneous groups by grouping together those products that require a similar, highly automated process; those that require a manual, high-precision process; those that are usually manufactured in very long series and distributed from stock; those that, in contrast, are manufactured in very short series to order and with a very high margin; etc. It is not possible to give a priori a set number of categories but, for many complex factories, between three and five main groups are usually sufficient to produce a substantial improvement.

These homogeneous groups can be obtained using industrial criteria or competitive strategy criteria. In the former case, greater consideration will be paid to aspects of homogeneity in the way the products are made and, in the latter case, the emphasis will be placed on how they are used to compete in the market.

Skinner says that, in each homogeneous group, it is necessary to identify a few aspects of crucial importance that must be

---

* Wickham Skinner was a Harvard Business School professor and the creator of productive ideas on the organization of industrial manufacture. See, for example, his books and articles listed in the Bibliography.

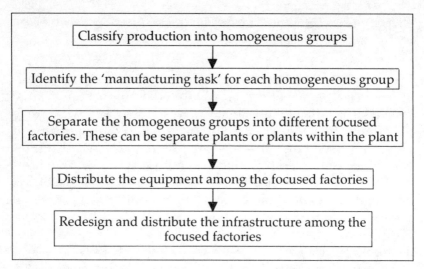

Figure 4.2 *Process of organizing production by focused factories*

carried out well in order for the group to be manufactured efficiently and in order to be able to compete successfully. In one case, the key may be to achieve a very low cost; in another case, the priority may be to make production so flexible that it is possible to manufacture efficiently even just one unit of the product at any one time. These priority goals for each homogeneous group are called the 'manufacturing task' by Skinner.

The second step consists of physically separating production of these homogeneous groups, if possible, taking them physically from the large original factory and placing them in another plant somewhere else. As this is only possible in a very few cases, another alternative is to redistribute production in the plant, isolating the new groups that have been created by means of partitions. In the first case, we will have a new focused plant and, in the second case, we will have a focused plant within another plant.

In the third step, the equipment is allocated to the various focused plants. More often than not, there is not enough equipment to go round because when all the production was mixed together in the large plant, all the equipment was shared by all the production. The method of creating focused factories usually requires an additional investment in equipment. This additional investment is fully justified by the improvements obtained in efficiency.

The fourth step consists of redesigning and distributing the production infrastructure in accordance with the needs of each focused plant. By production infrastructure, we mean the systems on which the production processes are based: scheduling, task design, quality, maintenance, training, control, etc. In a large factory, the same systems are used to organize and control the entire volume of operations. In a factory organized by focused units, each unit has its own systems, usually simpler, and always closer to the operations themselves and more matched to their characteristics. Thus, it may be that in one focused unit the key criterion is maintenance due to the high degree of automation, while in another unit the key criterion is training due to the need for worker polyvalency and the heterogeneity of the products manufactured.

The concept of the focused factory seeks to replace complex, generic systems not related to the product manufactured or to its contribution to the company's competitiveness, with a series of simpler and more specific systems, customized to a subgroup of products and perfectly adapted both to production requirements and to marketing priorities. The aim is thus to imbue production with a philosophy in which simplicity and clarity of objectives predominate. Production managers know what they must pursue at any one time and the task of production management is decentralized and taken to where the action is.

The other production system design model we are going to explore is the flexible industrial model. One of my first assignments when I commenced my career as a business management teacher was to write up a series of case studies on a textile company located near Gerona at the end of the 1960s.* HICONSA had vertically integrated itself from rag recycling to fabric innovation. It obtained the fibre from the rags, then wove, dyed, knitted and finished them, carrying out all these stages for a wide range of winter and summer fabrics. To coordinate all this

---

* Case studies available in the IESE's case study library as P- 218 HICONSA (A), P-225 HICONSA (B), P-239 HICONSA (C), and P-246 HICONSA (D).

73

was a highly difficult task and, despite operating with large stocks between stages and trying to forecast the most important stages with qualified people in charge of coordination, the products came on to the market with considerable deficiencies both in quantity and in time and cost. HICONSA did not survive for very long and I remember that when those case studies were discussed, many students concluded that the textile industry was better suited to countries with very low costs as, given the enormous complexity of the textile process, it would never be possible to make the grade in quality, novelty, lead-times, price and quantity at European costs.

However, in the 1980s and 1990s, we see that some European and North American textile companies continue to be able to compete successfully, some of them even in spite of high levels of vertical integration. A well-studied example of this is Benetton.* This Italian multinational has been able to implement superbly the model of a flexible company capable of achieving relatively low costs. Benetton also starts from the wool and cotton fibre, weaves, knits, dyes and finishes, fashions, distributes and sells. The novelty lies in that, in each of these stages, Benetton only carries out part—sometimes a small part—of the work and the rest is done by external subcontractors. Thus, most of the weaving, knitting, fashioning and distribution is performed by the company's subcontractors, who are sometimes structured on two or three levels: subcontractor, subcontractor's subcontractor and so on. Most of the sales are made through the franchised shop system.

As Figure 4.3 shows, for each activity in the company's value added chain, it is possible to depict the percentage of that value's total value that is performed in-house (in the company's workshops, with personnel employed by the company, with its own warehouses, own transport equipment or own shops) and the percentage that is produced using outside resources

---

* Several case studies have been written about Benetton, two of them are available in the IESE's case study library as BENETTON (A) P-600 and BENETTON (B) P-601.

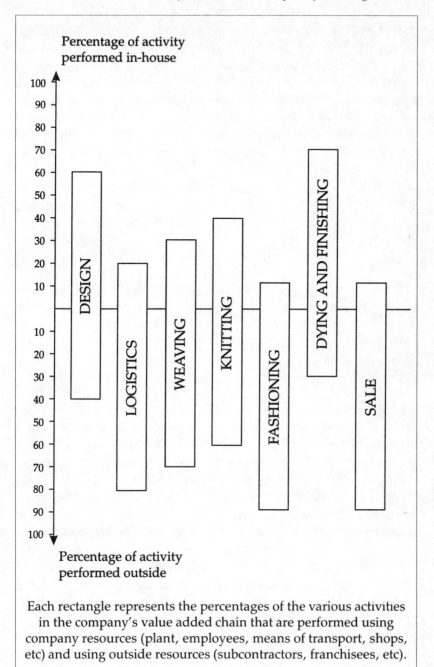

Each rectangle represents the percentages of the various activities in the company's value added chain that are performed using company resources (plant, employees, means of transport, shops, etc) and using outside resources (subcontractors, franchisees, etc).

Figure 4.3 *Diagram of a flexible design company*

(subcontracted workshops, purchased services, franchised shops). Obviously, the larger the part of the rectangle underneath the horizontal axis, the lesser is the company's commitment in that phase—in other words, the investments, the management problems, the responsibility for performance, all lie with the subcontractor. For the same reason, the company is more flexible. As is logical, the company will seek to ensure that the part of the activity that is performed in-house will guide and control what is done outside—that is, it will perform in-house that which is most critical or most differentiating.

In the event that competitive conditions vary substantially (fall in the demand, change in customers' tastes), the company that has implemented the type of system described above passes on to the subcontractors part of the variations imposed by the market, thus enabling it to adapt more easily to such variations. The network formed by the group of subcontractors is able to absorb the impact of this change by spreading it through its various levels. The network is more flexible than if the entire system was placed under the same roof. The network composed of the company and its subcontractors, franchisees and service providers contains a multitude of supplier–customer relationships. All of these relationships are governed by the market laws of supply and demand and it is these laws that stimulate efficiency. If the thousands of workers that work for Benetton were all under the same roof as Benetton employees, the company would have to recruit hundreds of middle managers to control these employees, they would probably be unionized and their negotiating power would be enormous. In such conditions, the company would never be able to function.

There are other companies like Benetton. The Spanish company Camper, a market leader in many segments of the footwear industry, came into being like Benetton, using a flexible approach. Other companies have adopted conventional approaches and were able to turn around by evolving towards this type of model. Thus, Sáez Merino, SA, a vertically integrated textile company known above all for its jeans brand Lois—one of Spain's classic brands—had chosen the integrated model in the 1960s and 1970s: almost all the production was carried out by personnel employed by the company in its own factories. The decline of jeans as a fashion item, the proliferation of brands and the market demands for a greater variety of sportswear brought the industrial rigidity into direct conflict with the demand for flexibility. Under the leadership of a production man like Manuel Sáez Merino, the company's founder and president, the company was able to restructure itself during the 1980s, achieving a greater flexibility by means of the implementation of concepts such as those we have analysed in the previous pages. However, in the early stages of the collision between rigid supply and demand requiring flexibility, the company had to resort to temporary layoffs with considerable frequency. Olivetti is another company which, under the leadership of Carlo de Benedetti, has also been able to achieve flexibility in a large part of its operations in order to overcome its crisis.

Coordination with another company

Compete and cooperate seem to be watchwords in the fight for holding positions in the European market. Europe has a very large, well-supplied market in a small surface area. In such conditions, the Spanish sell (or try to sell) in Germany and the Germans sell (without so many problems) in Spain. Whether we choose to or not, we are rubbing shoulders with our competitors every day. So why throw away money that one has to work so hard to earn by doing things inefficiently? Let us suppose that Thyssen in Germany manages to sell a certain hot-rolled steel coil to Volkswagen for its Pamplona plant while Altos Hornos de Vizcaya manages to sell exactly the same product to MAN for its plant near Munich. What would there be to prevent Altos Hornos from delivering to Pamplona and Thyssen to Munich? Nothing, it would appear, and both companies would save significant transportation and logistics costs. Actual reality is not so simple, although this type of coordination does happen. Where does coordination end and monopolistic practice begin? There is no clear dividing line. European cement manufacturers must know a lot about coordination because many people think of them with envy when the subject is discussed.

The petrochemical industry also knows how to coordinate. In the course of the restructuring of the European petrochemical industry during the 1980s,* several companies carried out swaps consisting of exchanging plants in order to improve their efficiency and competitiveness. Thus, for example, ICI and British Petroleum competed with each other and with other companies in the polyethylene and PVC sectors. ICI was strong in PVC and weak in polyethylene, while BP was strong in polyethylene and weak in PVC. Both companies sat down to negotiate and swapped their capacities with the result that BP abandoned PVC and ICI abandoned polyethylene while at the same time both companies came out stronger *vis-à-vis* other competitors in the other sector.

In Spain, in early 1991, Marcial Ucin and the CELSA Group carried out a swap whereby CELSA transferred 50 per cent of the ownership of Esteban Orbegozo to Marcial Ucin, which had the other 50 per cent, and Marcial Ucin assigned to CELSA 100 per cent of Siderúrgica del Besós. The Esteban Orbegozo plant was located very close to Marcial Ucin (in Guipúzcoa); consequently, if Marcial Ucin could acquire full ownership of it, it could rationalize both plants—as a single unit—with a series of major advantages. For its part, Siderúrgica del Besós was located near CELSA, both were in Barcelona, and it was also possible to achieve a significant degree of rationalization between these two plants. The swap enabled both projects to be brought to fruition, increasing the competitiveness of all four plants and both companies. Aside from the fact that they have been able to come to an agreement to carry out the swap, Marcial Ucin and the CELSA Group are renowned for being 'no holds barred' competitors.†

This coordination can also take place between supplier and customer. A supplier–customer integration reduces inventory,

---

* This process has been described in an excellent manner by Joseph Bower in his book *When Markets Quake*.
† The ACENOR series of case studies referred to previously shows one aspect of the competition between these two groups in their fight to gain control of ACENOR.

improves service, makes it easier to organize production, and also offers other profit-increasing benefits. The supplier no longer continually has to go out to the market to win over its customers, with no certainty as to the latter's continuity. By integrating with the customer, the supplier must open up to receive information, it must be prepared to invest (in R & D, in equipment) in what its customer is interested in. The relationship has been called 'partenariat'* or 'co-manufacturing'.† This type of coordination between supplier and customer may be useful in helping companies or divisions in a position of relative weakness to continue if it manages to convince the customer of the advantages of a supplier willing to become an effective, long-term business associate.

THE TURNAROUND TIMETABLE

A turnaround process is a race against time. In a declining company, the situation is deteriorating with each minute that passes. Turning around a company requires acting in the right direction even though the uncertainty and lack of information mean that some actions will be very productive and others will go by virtually unnoticed. But one cannot afford to lose time. One cannot let the water keep coming in.

At any one time, the trees may obscure the wood because there are a thousand and one problems and, for the person who has been commissioned with carrying out the turnaround, everything is new. It is important to discern what is really important from what seems to be important to others and to not have any qualms in postponing or completely forgetting about whatever is not crucial.

The most useful tool in this process is the timetable, the specific PERT timetable that the turnaround manager has drawn

---

* Partenariat in the sense of partners in a project. Companies such as Renault and General Motors Europe have developed specific models of action for implementing this type of supplier—customer integration.
† Co-manufacturing is the North American version of partenariat and also means the willingness to share in the customer's risks and advantages.

79

up for himself. The timetable is closely related with the cash plan, which is the second major tool. Between them, these two tools set what must be done, who must do it, when it must be done by and how much it affects the flow of funds.

The timetable and its projection to improve the flow of funds should be so clear that no one in the management team involved in the process has any doubts about the objectives that must be achieved in order to advance in the right direction.

If the turnaround is to become a reality, then the new, unconventional things that are going to be done and which will change the situation must have been identified. Sometimes, some of these things would be included in what we could call 'penny pinching',* but that is not enough. All managers should inculcate a penny-pinching policy in their company (and all fathers in their homes), no matter how unpopular it might be. However, the fact of the matter is that these policies are formally implemented when things are going bad and are forgotten when things are going well. Therefore, penny-pinching should be an ongoing policy and not subject to a timetable.

The turnaround timetable must include important, difficult and sometimes painful actions the harshness of which had prevented them from being implemented until now: a temporary layoff of part of the workforce, refinancing, staff cuts, sale of properties, strengthening of a sales network, closure of part of the business, etc. Each of these actions should be completed by a certain time and a person should be appointed who accepts the task and undertakes to carry it out.

THE TOLERANCE OF THE STAKEHOLDERS

As we have explained in a previous chapter, the decline of a company is a process of collective self-deception. Everyone knows that the situation is terrible but no one wants to be the first to stick his neck out. In August 1991, a group

---

* Small actions that produce small savings—'Look after the pennies and the pounds look after themselves', etc. Less couriers, less faxes and more normal letters, less subscriptions, hotels with one star less, take out to dinner only the customers who are going to buy, etc.

of commercial and savings banks sued the Dutch company Akzo to force it to accept responsibility for paying the loans granted to its Spanish subsidiary La Seda de Barcelona. However, the subsidiary's problems, in an industrial climate of deep depression, had been common knowledge for some time. Probably while the sick but not yet 'officially sick'* company's loans and debts continued to be refinanced, everyone must have thought, 'It's too important for it to really be a risk', or perhaps, 'We're not the only ones in this, so-and-so is in it too.' But when it was decided that the company was 'officially sick', then everybody rushed to ask for their money back.

This is an additional and rather strange problem that the turnaround team must cope with. The previous management, the ones who created the black hole, the ones who ruined the company, were able to benefit from the self-deception of banks, unions, suppliers and authorities, who thus became accomplices to the failure. However, when the turnaround team arrives, it finds everyone up in arms: the banks want their loans back and are not even prepared to give the financing they had granted previously, the suppliers want to collect the money owed to them and be paid in cash on delivery from now on, the unions say that they will not accept any staff cuts because it is unacceptable, and the customers, jumping on the bandwaggon, delay payments and return the part of their purchase that they are not able to use.

Any team intending to successfully turn around a company or business unit must first obtain the confidence of the parties involved. If there is no reasonableness† on the part of all those involved, then there is no solution to the problem. However, there is still some reasonableness, especially in the business world, and confidence in the turnaround team may be created if it either has sufficient credentials or is good at putting up convincing arguments. Whatever may be the clinching

---

* We could say that a company is 'officially sick' when the press says so. These days, the power of the press in the economy and business is so great that we could be justified in assigning it this responsibility.

† According to the philosophers, reasonableness is seeing things as they are.

argument used, experience has shown that on many occasions, banks, suppliers, customers, unions and government have been tolerant with a group of managers to help them put an ailing company back on its feet. As we will discuss in a later chapter, turning around a company is a process of agreements. Considerable negotiating skills must be deployed with a view to obtaining a series of agreements. Once everyone is agreed, it is possible to act.

CONCLUSION

Without doubt, the most satisfying job that any manager can do is to turn around a declining company by revitalizing its components and avoiding major surgery. This must be so because most of the people who manage it either write a book on it or get someone else to write a book on it. And that considering that senior managers do not like writing and most of them write very poorly. For them—and for European academics—writing is an unprofitable activity.

To decide on this approach, the manager must feel that the company still has enough life in it to make it worthwhile trying to maintain the complete entity, without having to resort to cutting up and transplanting before the organs start to rot. Discovering what that minimum quantity of life necessary is, is still an art, and although without doubt it would a good subject for a PhD thesis, I fear it will be many years yet before someone writes it.

Once on the way towards the objective, there are a number of models that can be followed, from adjusting conservatively to expanding audaciously, including the search for more flexible corporate designs. The choice will depend on the circumstances of the general economic situation, of the company and of the management team. The various alternatives have common features that allow them to be grouped in the categories we have analysed in this chapter.

5

The moment of truth

T he title of Chapter 2 was 'The capacity for self-deception'. We attributed the deterioration of a company to the capacity to maintain a prolonged deception. However, when it comes to revitalizing the company, at some time the truth must be made known and the deception is revealed for what it is. Sometimes, only the people inside the company are caught in the deception. Sometimes, even the press may hit on the truth. However, there comes a time when it is as if everyone agrees to admit the real state of affairs.

WHO ADMITS THE TRUTH?

A n interesting question we could ask is 'Who decides that the truth must come out?' Generally, they are not the same people as have prolonged the deception. When Jan Timmer was appointed president of Philips in the early 1990s, he decided that 40,000 people would have to be made redundant between 1990 and 1992 and the company would have to pull out of a large number of divisions. Obviously, the problem had not appeared overnight. Philips' decline started many years before and continued during the term of office of some previous president. When General Motors decided to close its Lynne factory, it was not because its productivity had dropped off in the weeks prior to the decision. When the Ministry of Industry and Energy and the INI decided in 1990 to privatize the heavy vehicles manufacturer Pegaso, it was not precisely because they considered it the jewel in the crown in the stock of state-controlled companies. Pegaso had been gradually declining since the 1970s but other INI presidents and other Ministers of Industry did not act. When, during this privatization process, the first deal with MAN-Daimler Benz fell through and a sale was rushed through to the Fiat Group at a symbolic price, it was because someone, perhaps the Minister of Industry himself or the president of INI, realized that what was once a profitable company at that time was virtually worthless. When Tom Plaskett, the President of Pan Am expressed in late 1990 his willingness first to sell his most profitable North Atlantic routes to United Airlines and later to merge his company with the also ailing TWA, he was no doubt aware that he could not go on much longer with a declining market share and growing indebtedness. A lot had changed in the air transport industry since the years when Pan Am was the first company to link the United States with the rest of the world by air, and while companies like American Airlines, United and Delta were gaining ground year by year, Pan Am had been losing it. The package of decisions taken by the management of Saab Scania regarding their activity in automobile manufacture (deinvestment in components and industrial agreements with General Motors) was probably the result of their recognition of the truth that it might not be possible to continue as an independent automobile manufacturer with a major contribution of in-house technology in a demand segment in which it had only a small market share worldwide.

The expression 'moment of truth' has been used on innumerable occasions as a metaphor to refer to the time when the condemned prisoner must face his sentence, a bullfighter must kill the bull, a soldier must fight the enemy, or many other occasions when a person cannot put off any longer facing a situation about which he may have entertained more or less realistic prospects, illusions, fantasies, false hopes or self-deception. In the life of the company, as we have seen from the above examples, there also comes a time when one must face the reality of the decline and start the turnaround. During the processes of decline, there are sometimes changes in the top management but the new managers do not always face the challenge of acknowledging the truth. A very large company or a state-owned company may have sufficient inertia to survive for many years in a gradual decline. But inexorably, one day the deception must stop and that is the moment of truth for the decaying company.

There is no problem in telling when a company is on the way down. We have offered ways of showing this in Chapter 2. However, it is not so easy to tell when a company is near the point of no return. There are managers who are able to portray a company's failure as a success. Saddam Hussein's ability not to acknowledge his defeat to the citizens of his country has its parallels in the business world. On the other hand, to operate on a company that does not need it because it is simply going through a trough would be a serious mistake.

One needs a certain sixth sense to judge the degree of irreversibility of the situation of decline. But this sixth sense can be backed by an aggressive and realistic diagnosis. A company that manufactured basic materials for pharmacy and veterinary medicine was suffering from a marked deterioration in its results due to the maturity of its products, which had become commodities. As a result of this situation, certain changes were made in the company's management. The new general manager found himself with a new plant that was being built to manufacture a certain substance. The company's entire management team trusted that as soon as the new plant was started up, the situation would take a remarkable turn for the better. However, after a rapid objective analysis, the new manager concluded that the new substance that would be manufactured there was basically another commodity and that the new plant was neither technologically innovative nor optimally sized and, therefore, that the company was in a serious fix. He immediately put the project on hold to reduce expenses and implemented a drastic austerity plan as the starting points for a turnaround process. In cases like that, there are always people who criticize that the situation was not that bad, that if time was given to a series of projects things would work out, that a firm base needs a long-term perspective, etc. It is difficult to prove who is right.

THE PROFILE OF THE LEADER

Lee Iaccocca of Chrysler, Jan Carlzon of SAS, Mario Schimberni of Montedison, Carlo de Benedetti of Olivetti, John Harvey-Jones of ICI, Claudio Boada of the Banco Hispano Americano, Luis Magaña of FECSA and Alfredo Sáez of Banca Catalana are characters who can be associated with well-known turnarounds, who were successful at a particular point in time, with a certain degree of support from the economic situation in some cases as their critics would add, but who had the undoubted merit that, in several cases, has led to their efforts being immortalized in print. Without doubt, they are all very different people. However, all of them share a common feature, which is the acceptance of publicity and, in some cases, even inviting it. Consequently, it would not be completely correct to deduce the profile of the entrepreneur able to turn around companies from the cases that have received the most limelight. Turning around a large company in trouble can hardly be a confidential task, the public turnarounders might argue, but the fact is that there have been people who have been able to achieve great feats while keeping a very low profile. It may perhaps be useful to approach the profile of this type of entrepreneur from a less direct angle, identifying some of the abilities that such people possess to a greater extent than other businessmen and women.

It is difficult or rash to approach any problem without putting it into a suitable perspective: define the time gap within which events may take place; quantify all the various types of resources required (human, managerial, financial, technical); anticipate the complications that might arise; limit the possible reactions of the various stakeholders; forecast the evolution of the general situation within the project's life cycle and its possible repercussion on its execution. To take in this highly complex reality riddled with uncertainty and correctly size it, no matter how tentatively, is a very rare skill. However, an analysis of the way in which managers work on company turnaround projects shows that they often refer to their mental construct of the project they are involved in and the estimated size they have assigned to it.

Once the problem has been sized, one must prepare and motivate the effort to solve it. A small group of very able and highly motivated executives can deploy an enormous total effort, much greater than that of an army of uncoordinated and disheartened managers. However, a company turnaround usually has components that have a life and timetable of their own. Political processes such as general, regional or union elections may impose their pace, administrative processes that must comply with the deadlines and circumstances provided for by law, processes affecting the workforce such as temporary layoffs, naturally slow down the pace in the management of the turnaround. Therefore, one must maintain a balance between the effort applied, the size of the problem and the right speed. One of the consequences of this is the necessity of being able to define the team required.

Some self-titled turnarounders boast of being lone operators, with just a telephone and a secretary. This is not usually the case. They are always backed by a team of perhaps unsung heroes but who nevertheless do the work. It is true that there are good orchestra conductors who outshine excellent virtuosos but the best conductor in the world, gesticulating alone on a podium without any orchestra to conduct even though it is hidden in the proscenium, in the darkness of a large opera house, would be laughed off the stage.

Of the two turnaround categories discussed in this book, revitalization or multiple transplant, the former usually requires more effort and, therefore, more teamwork than the latter. Perhaps it is also a more enriching and noble task.

Choosing the human team that will work on the turnaround is a great art and is perhaps the most valuable skill of the people who triumph in this type of project. It is not difficult to identify people who, either as managers or as consultants, followed leaders such as Claudio Boada, Mario Chimberni, Carlo de Benedetti and others in more than one project. Others have a well-defined and balanced team, with specific tasks — finance, legal affairs, labour aspects, etc — which they use to tackle certain projects, replacing them with 'conventional' executives as the problem clarifies. Perhaps this is the style of Javier de la Rosa and Giovanni Agnelli. Some are able to identify in the struggling company they are going to turn around the team of people who are going to work with them, and are able to practically transform these people, drawing from them energy and resources to a degree that even they themselves were not aware they had, for example, Volkswagen, with a few people from Seat's team such as Díaz Alvarez or Díaz Ruiz, Miguel Canalejo of Alcatel with people from the old Standard, John Harvey-Jones when he was at ICI.

Table 5.1 *Skills of the revitalizing leader*

Analytic skills	• Ability to size the problem
	  – Structure of the problem
	  – Stakeholders
	  – Situation in the general context
	  – Progress timetable
	• Ability to measure effort
	  – Economic resources available or mobilizable
	  – Managerial resources available or recruitable
	  – Technical resources available or obtainable

Interpersonal skills	• Selection of management team • Motivation of management team • Maintenance of management team
Emotional skills	• Self-control • Negotiating skill • Ability to inspire confidence

The leader we are studying must also not only have a great emotional capacity and a strong personality but also a great self-control and an enormous ability to direct himself in acting the most appropriate part at any one time. He must be a skilful negotiator as a turnaround is based on a large number of agreements. Only a great emotional strength can enable him to keep a cool head when everything is tottering and it is the leader's calmness that keeps the team fighting, that inspires trust in those who might contribute to the process's success (bankers, politicians, union leaders, customers, suppliers).

Table 5.1 provides a summary of the skills or abilities of the type of manager we have referred to as a revitalizing leader.

THE TURNAROUND COMMANDO

B ringing together a team of powerful executives, balancing it, motivating it, directing it during long periods of high stress and, retaining it is not an easy task. Most of these executives have options to work in other places. All of them pass through times of doubt when they wonder what they are doing there, running an enormous risk and under great stress when— tomorrow if they wanted—they could be having a quieter time in any other job. As someone has defined, it is like going to fight at the front with an army of volunteers who had the option to back out at any time. During a turnaround process, it is commonplace for the managers involved to have to work fifteen or sixteen hours every day, work Saturdays and Sundays, travel constantly, expect telephone calls at any time. If the company has several centres affected by the project, the amount of travelling obviously increases, with the resulting increase in the stress created by the experience of travelling itself and the fear of arriving late. Keeping suitcases with spare clothes in the boot of the car parked at the airport; knowing the telephone number of regularly used taxi companies or that have vehicles with a telephone; priority bought in restaurants with private dining- rooms; sleeping pills; double reservations on alternative flights; family life in shreds; interminable dinners with wearing negotia- tions; total and permanent tension to catch the hint, decide whether or not to answer the telephone, adopt an unbending or flexible attitude; a willingness to make more effort than the others, more initiative, more work — all this is part and parcel of life in a turnaround.

Managing a human team that is living in these conditions is like sitting on a fragile cart pulled by a galloping group of warhorses. To keep managers at full pace while preventing them from fighting with each other, losing heart, opting for self-protection or confining themselves to defending their bit of territory requires an enormous capacity for feedback to work out what is going on, provide a rapid and accurate diagnosis and immediately correct the tension on each of the reins.

To bring together a group of superexecutives, all of them new, to carry out a turnaround project is exceedingly rash. Most successful turnarounds made use of a large number of managers who were already in the company or who came from companies in the same industry linked with the project leader. Even in those cases which have stressed the leader's ability to achieve extraordinary results from people who were new in the project and of whom he had no previous knowledge, it is possible to find a few key people who had been working with the leader since long before. This is the case of Kenneth Iverson who is attributed with having proved that it is possible to turn around not only a steel company but the entire US steel industry.* There is no doubt that Mr Iverson is a great leader and that he has had the courage to assign key functions in his Nuccor project to recently recruited people, many of them unfamiliar with the industry. However, the careful observer will note the presence of a small core of assistants who have been with Kenneth Iverson since the beginnings of his crusade to demature† an industry.

It is vital that the leader of a turnaround project feel that he is truly in control of his team. Under the duress of the process, there may be desertions, mutinies and even betrayals. The terrible pace of the process may lead people to justify to

---

* O Kenneth Iverson is either a genius in handling public relations or is a rare case of a person who has been well treated by media who are usually little inclined to be generous. In 1991, Richard Preston published his book *American Steel* which was basically a panegyric to the leader able to revitalize the rust belt. Subsequently, the prestigious journal *The New Yorker* reproduced the book virtually in its entirely in two successive issues in early 1991.

† The concept 'demature' has been used to define those situations in which innovative ways are found to manufacture a mature product, thus pushing it back to an earlier stage in the product's life cycle (higher margin and possibility of quick sales growth).

themselves actions that to an outside observer would seem unjustifiable. But for the entire team to be loyal, all of its members must feel the support of the leader and his closest assistants. An executive who has been locked in a plant by its workers, whose name has been mentioned in the press as being accused by the workers of wanting to put hundreds of bread-winners out of work, who is giving his word to banks and suppliers, must feel supported by the leader and his immediate assistants. If the leader falters, then he should not be surprised if that faithful executive becomes his enemy.

Between a leader and his team there is a kind of potential differential which is the sum of a series of differentials in personality, prestige, power, ability to reward and punish, and negotiating skills. The greater this differential is the easier it will be for the leader to control his team. If there are people who have been working with the leader for some time, it will be easier for the leader to fine tune his control. People recruited *ex profeso* for the project may cause a few surprises.

THE COMPENSATION OF THE TEAM

The leaders of these processes use many ways to motivate their team. In general, this type of work is well paid. It is sometimes surprising to see the kind of money that people working in corporate turnarounds can earn. As it is usually not acceptable to grant very high salaries in such circumstances, sometimes the teams working in these projects are paid through consultancies or management companies, sometimes they are remunerated in the form of shares or holdings, or they are authorized to carry out parallel business operations that can be performed as part of the turnaround (a commission for selling an asset, an extra remuneration through the board of a certain subsidiary, a share in a new company created by spinning off a certain activity as a separate company, etc.), or they are promised success fees or special bonuses which they will be paid if everything goes well. The promise may be a high-level post in the restructured company.

Taking part in the project may sometimes have an intrinsic appeal, in spite of the effort and risk and irrespective of the remuneration. There is the visibility obtained *vis-à-vis* the communications media and influential people who may appreciate these managers' skills and be interested in using them at some later point in one of their projects. There is the possibility of including in one's résumé a series of major achievements (reducing a workforce by 500 people, renegotiating £40 million of debt, closing a production centre, selling an important asset, etc). For many executives, whose preoccupations go beyond the frivolous aspects of taking part in this type of project, there is the experience of being able to increase one's personal enrichment in a short period of time with unforgettable experiences whose very intensity forges professionalism. Some executives say that it has been worthwhile fighting to save a company which, without their effort, would surely have gone under. But that is easily said and yet it is very difficult to determine what percentage of heroism is contained in the effort. Most leaders who have had to lead teams of executives in turnaround projects assure that they have found very few heroes.

Jean-Claude was the general manager of a medium-sized precision-engineered plastic parts factory in Lyon. At his age, 35 years, the job was a magnificent achievement and the remuneration was very attractive. However, the company had a controlling owner who was 60 years old, who was active in the company and took part in any important decision and, what was worse, a 21-year-old son who seemed to be bright and was destined to replace his father one day. Jean-Claude could have a very pleasant life for five, perhaps up to ten years; the company was doing well and no problems were in the offing. However, Jean-Claude's ambition kept driving him on and he finally accepted the risk of joining a group of managers that were planning a leveraged buyout of a division of a large chemical company that was being restructured.

The project required that he put into it most of his savings. The division could be purchased relatively cheaply but they would start with very high debt levels. They would have to work extremely hard because the division had three plants of which one or two would have to be closed, transferring part of the production to the third. The workforce would have to be reduced. If everything went well, the reorganized division could be sold or listed on the stock market, which could give him a very high capital gain on his investment.

Jean-Claude knew that he would have to spend his life travelling between Paris and the towns in the South-East where the plants of the division to be restructured were located. He would spend few nights at home, in spite of the excellent connection by high speed train between Paris and Lyon. Financially speaking, his monthly salary would be lower but if everything went well, he could retire in a couple of years. Jean-Claude was married and had two daughters, aged three and five. His wife had an interesting job in the Ministry of Education in Lyon. All of his and his wife's close family lived in Lyon. He thought of taking his family to Paris. That way he could spend a few more hours with them. But breaking up his wife's career and leaving her on her own, shut in an *appartement* in Paris, hoping to get a government job there (where there was 'overstaffing') was no solution.

The leveraged buyout project was led by a young, well-known executive who had held high-level posts in the government and in state-controlled companies during the Fabius period and he had performed brilliantly in all his assignments. Jean-Claude had had some contact with him as a supplier, in negotiating the refinancing of a debt against his company, and both men had liked each other. Also, both had studied in the HEC.* The 'tycoon' had good memories of Jean-Claude and needed someone with a strong technical-industrial base in plastics. Jean-Claude knew that working with this genius would be exciting but he also knew that it would make him known and admired in French business circles.

These days, the Jean-Claude syndrome is one of the commonest diseases among young executives. What in the past

---

* HEC (Hautes Etudes Commerciales), Centre HEC-ISA, Chambre de Commerce et d'Industrie de Paris, with headquarters in Jouy-en-Josas, France. It is one of France's elite management schools.

must have been the merchants, adventurers and explorers, who travelled to strange lands hoping for great profit in exchange for risk and danger are today those young men in dark suits, Yves Saint Laurent suitcases and Hermés ties that you can find in all the airports of the world early Monday morning, urgently leaving for some temporary destination where there await enormous challenges, gigantic possibilities and heaps of work.

Of all the forms of remunerating executives taking part in a turnaround project, that which this author recommends is the combination of a good fixed salary and a bonus on the result, so that the fixed salary comprises the largest part of the package. For example, if we are talking about a large-scale project and experienced managers in the key stage of their career (35 to 45 years), we could suggest a fixed salary between £125,000 and £200,000 gross per annum and a bonus, which can be broken down into annual stages as the project advances, of about another £100,000 per annum. Table 5.2 shows a possible remuneration based on the size of the unit to be turned around.

Table 5.2 *Guidelines for manager remuneration in turnaround process*

Sales turnover	Gross annual remuneration £000	Gross annual bonus £000
1,000 to 5,000	40– 75	15– 25
5,000 to 10,000	50–125	25– 50
10,000 to 25,000	100–175	50–100
25,000 to 50,000	125–200	75–125

It should be understood that we are talking about 'proven' executives and a successful turnaround. Obviously, sales are a variable that only suggests one dimension but, depending on the industry, the figures should be adjusted to match the complexity; £5 million in textile fashioning represents infinitely more complexity than £5 million in cement sales. These figures should be considered with extreme caution, as a mere guideline, based on a number of data referring to 1991. In any case, they are

The moment of truth

figures for the key managers in the process who, depending on the project's complexity, may number between two and five people.

Let us suppose that we have a group of three managers who are turning around a division with annual sales of £125 million and whose fixed salaries average £150,000. Let us suppose that we expect to progress from heavy losses to zero profit in one year and from zero net profit to 5 per cent of sales in another year (this 5 per cent being an acceptable figure in the industry). Let us suppose that a bonus is set for fulfilling these objectives amounting to £75,000 in the first year and £100,000 in the second year, on average, keeping the base salary fixed for both years. Once the turnaround has been achieved, part of the annual bonus can be put into the fixed salary and the other part can be restructured. This can either consist of discontinuing it, considering the exceptional nature of the effort required during the turnaround period, or include it in a new bonus based on other objectives. Thus, for example, in this illustration, the managers could increase their base salary to an average of £200,000 gross and a bonus of £25,000 or £50,000 linked with an improvement in net profit, a reduction in stocks and an improvement in market share, for example.

An employer or board of directors, at the time of crisis when the company is collapsing around them, may be prepared to offer enormous salaries and astronomic bonuses. The problem is then to bring such situations back down to normal. After paying a bonus of £500,000 how can one then offer £125,000 per annum to a manager, once we are back to normal? Another consideration is how much more does a bonus of £150,000 motivate than a bonus of £100,000? Anyone who can define the difference must be a genius in human understanding.

Turnaround processes burn out managers. They burn them out for many reasons: because of the stress, because of failure, because of the politics that sometimes infects the project. But they can also be burned out by success and this is a factor which should be considered together with the analysis of the remuneration.

CASE STUDIES

A management team commissioned to reorganize a seriously ill company controlled by a bank was promised by this bank that, in the event of success, their bonus would be the amount of the interest that the heavily indebted company owed to the bank. The task included separating the company from the bank, solving the company's crisis and paying back the bank its loans. The bank's senior management probably thought that the task was impossible and therefore that they would never be called upon to honour the payment. However, the executives did a marvellous job and fulfilled all the objectives. When it came to the crunch, the bank's managers were not clear in their acknowledgement of the remuneration and the administrative obstacles that came in the way were such that in the end the executives never received this bonus. The ambiguity of the situation led some of the stakeholders to doubt the executives' right to the remuneration and what had been a spectacular piece of crisis management became overshadowed by these circumstances.

One employer convinced one of his managers to accept responsibility for reorganizing a division. The project required a severe staff reduction, negotiating the refinancing of a number of debts with several banks and suppliers, exchanging part of the debt for certain assets and rebuilding a disintegrating sales network by attracting good salesmen and forming alliances with distributors. The employer offered very high bonuses for the various phases of the process. In order to keep him motivated, he also accepted including the manager as partner in some of the joint ventures created to regain the market. Over a period of three years, the manager earned over £1.25 million (1988–1991). The manager did a good job but got used to negotiating with the employer as one partner to another and offered to coinvest his money in the opportunities that arose for the reorganized company. There came a time when the employer was no longer sure that his manager was maximizing the division's or his own results. There was no way that the situation could be downscaled and the employer had to let the manager go after paying a considerable severance payment and replace him.

An employer that owned several companies replaced the general manager of a building material distributor that was in serious difficulties. The new manager, recruited in 1985, was a 36-year-old executive, and engineer with an MBA and 10 years' experience. He was offered a modest salary and a 10 per cent share in the company. Five years later and after the construction boom, in the late 1980s, the company not only had been turned around but had increased its sales fourfold and was making sizeable profits. The executive, who was still receiving his modest salary, saw in this 10 per cent the reward for his excellent management. In 1990, after speaking with an old teacher of his, the executive started to wonder, 'How much is 10 per cent of a company worth when the other 90 per cent belongs to a single person?' His technical knowledge enabled him to calculate various figures to arrive at the value of the company: net value, multiple of the last three years' average profit, net present value of the foreseeable net profits over the next five years, correlation with the valuation obtained in other similar recent transactions, etc. These valuations and others gave figures ranging between £3 million and £6 million. Our executive therefore thought that his bonus amounted to between £300,000 and £600,000.

He decided to make a try and he suggested to the employer that as the company's turnaround process was now complete, he wished to realize his 10 per cent and receive a salary more in line with his present situation (41 years of age, experience, achievements). The reply did not take him overly aback because his old teacher had predicted that, in such cases, the employer's answer was usually something ambiguous ranging from 'let me think about it' to 'now's not a good time for big outlays' and including 'you're going a bit fast, aren't you' and even 'we'll see'. However, the employer said that he had no objection to the second part, that is, bringing his salary into line with market rates. After consulting again with his old teacher, the executive concluded that his 'bonus' was partly forgotten in the employer's mind. If he pressured to receive it; he would cause a crisis and without doubt would get nothing. Following his old teacher's advice, he did not force a crisis but negotiated a formula for realizing his 10 per cent in annual instalments, in the form of bonuses for results obtained for the company (undertaking to return the 10 per cent for a symbolic price). Although he understood that he should not let it show, his frustration and disenchantment were enormous and he later commented to his old teacher that the company was suffocating him and if he found anything else that was interesting, he would not mind leaving, even at the cost of losing whatever else was owing to him.

We have seen three examples of how unspecific, poorly defined, insufficiently documented or excessive bonuses and shares in the company, offered in the heat of the battle without a clear exit route, may end up burning out or turning against the executives who take part in a turnaround, and how they may destabilize the relationship between such executives and the project's subsequent development. These considerations lead us precisely to our next point, the post-turnaround stage.

THE POST-TURNAROUND STAGE

T he management team that takes part in the turnaround is
not always the correct one to continue managing the
company in normal conditions. Day-to-day management
of a reorganized company requires a very different kind of
performance. Teams composed of people who work harmo-
niously together must be formed and nurtured; technological
capacities must be built; the company must be equipped with
systems for processing the information and controlling management, and these systems must be maintained and updated; the
company must minutely plan its deployment on the market,
with selective offers for specific segments, monitoring competitors, tracking customers and creating rapid response mechanisms. In short, the most sophisticated management skills and
concepts must be applied. In addition to being good managers,
these executives must put into practice an elaborate
professionalism.

There is no longer need to apply surgery every day, now one
has to act as a grand generalist, managing the right specialists.
Sometimes, after a complex operation, one returns full of
gratitude and trust to the master surgeon who performed the
operation, seeking advice and a solution to the uncomfortable
twinges that remain, only to find that he puts one off with a
smile and a slap on the back, 'You're fine, what you need is an
endocrinologist, or a dietician, or a physiotherapist, or . . .' It is
immediately clear that his skill is in cutting out pieces of diseased
intestine, precisely removing from the body's tissues that which
should never have grown there, putting in valves, screws,
connections, etc, but not in taking away giddy spells, sweating,
arrhythmias or slow digestions. The hour in the GP's office does
not command the same rates as the hour in the operating theatre
and it is in the operating theatre that the surgeon feels he is in his
element.

The same thing happens with executives. The company is
turned around—and then what? In some cases, the problem
comes to a head from the money side. There appears an
enormous urgency to turn into money those shares that were

given when they were worthless and now may be worth a lot. Suddenly, the cool and sensible industrial manager can think of nothing else except who will buy his shares and when. They are offered on the stock market immediately, and a buyer is feverishly sought. Pressures, valuations, arguments. The problem may come from outside. Another company in difficulties has spotted that executive who can no longer put into practice every day his marvellous skills and he receives an offer that is far higher than the salary that is paid for managing in normal cicumstances.

As we have seen in the previous section, remuneration may be a cause of serious problems once the company's activity returns to normal. There are more or less standard salaries in the market for each type of responsibility. For example, a good sales manager for a medium-sized company (£50 million in annual sales) manufacturing automobile components could command, in 1991, between £50,000 and £100,000 per annum. However, for the three or four executives that were able to turn around such a company when it was on the brink of disaster, the company may have had to pay £250,000 or 500,000, between one thing and another. How can one combine the second with the first?

After turning around a company, some managers choose to continue working part time. They have earned a lot of money and now set about administering it—and fairly often losing it. Some consider themselves entrepreneurs and start companies of their own or turn to the second oldest profession in the world: real estate development. A management post in a functional or general area in a healthy company does not give them fulfilment. To keep executives in the company part time is a mistake. It sets a very poor example and masks the fact that, deep down, that manager is not good at his job. Healthy companies, if they are to remain so, also need an enormous amount of attention and dedication.

Right from the start of a turnaround process, one must be aware that some of the executives involved will probably be lost in the process. Some of them may be appointed to higher levels of responsibility in the reorganized company and will continue. Others will accept the change of activity and will be able to adapt. However, some will not adapt and one must accept that they must go. All this requires a certain degree of planning. One must be careful when signing severance pay contracts. One must think twice before offering shares. One must avoid promising a certain position in the company, once restored to health, as a reward for the work done during the turnaround. Nobody can know how things will go and it is better to promise little than be forced to not keep promises.

The people taking part in a turnaround process live through a period of intense learning. Scholars of human learning accept that a little pressure is helpful. The pressure of the urgency and seriousness of the consequences that one is trying to avoid in a turnaround stimulate the development of many abilities in the people who live through the experience. It can be said that at the end of a successful turnaround, the company has a human team that is more able than when it began. However, managing a more able team also requires more skill and, if this is not forthcoming, the team is destroyed.

CONCLUSION

A situation of decline quickly contaminates anyone who tries to grapple with it. Even though when taking up a new position in a company of the type we are analysing here the managers who are there will play down the bad symptoms and emphasize the presentable aspects, one must subject the situation to a frank, objective and aggressive diagnosis and have the courage to admit that the moment of truth has come and something must be done to change the direction the company is headed in.

The people faced with a turnaround must be able to handle the scalpel with a steady hand and only cut away what is bad. The strengths that have been built up with years of effort and which provide a—sometimes intangible—reserve of future results must be protected. However, one must be able to distinguish between strengths and burdens and, in the event of doubt, remember that certain strengths that will produce results in the future will not be able to do so if there is no future.

The turnaround leader is a person able to make rapid diagnoses, correctly finding more than two-thirds of the major elements of a problem. An optimal diagnosis may take months. A good turnaround leader must be able to achieve a correct diagnosis of the basic aspects in a few weeks. In exchange for speed, he suboptimizes instead of optimizing. He must have the skills of any good manager but he must stand out above all for his negotiating skill, as a turnaround is a succession of agreements.

Lawrence Fouraker, who was dean of the Harvard Business School during the 1970s, used to say that the best test for measuring the worth of a manager is the quality of the human team he is able to gather around him. This is even more true in a turnaround process when time and the pressure of circumstances are working against him. Success is always the result of a team, a turnaround is never the task of a single person.

There are leaders who have achieved success with people who would seem unexceptional to anyone in comparison with the supermen with sophisticated résumés built around an MBA. The important thing is to achieve a good leader–team balance in which, as the Catalans say, people concentrate their effort on working,* not on politics or in fighting with each other.

In the section on remuneration, the conclusion is that it must be set with an eye on the future impact of the conditions that are agreed and on the possible conflicts that may be created. There is a world of difference between pre-and post-turnaround situations. Things that were worthless are suddenly worth a lot, while people continue to appear the same. Owners who before had nothing now have a lot, thanks to the intervention of a few people, or so some may think. To reward with shares, commissions or assets realizable under certain conditions or to tolerate parallel businesses may help to interest executives in difficult projects but may backfire in later stages. If one wishes to retain the turnaround team, one must seek balanced remuneration packages—generally with generous fixed and variable parts—

---

* 'Tot hom va a per feina': everyone concentrates on the job to be done.

that can be scaled down to normal remuneration levels in normal conditions. There is a certain stock of unemployed executives, who usually introduce themselves as consultants, who have been spoiled by the financial conditions obtained in a turnaround project. They are either not prepared to work at normal rates or people dare not propose a project to them for fear that they ask for too much money.

The circumstances within which a turnaround process takes place tend to burn out some of the executives that participate in the project. This effect may have an underlying pathological basis, in which case the executive affected may show signs of abnormal behaviour (frequent illnesses, inability to sleep, drinking, requests for part-time work), or may be caused by political reasons that lead the executive no longer to feel comfortable as part of the team. It is a common occurrence and should be avoided.

6

Winners and losers

The entry of Fiat in Pegaso, of Volkswagen in Seat, of Delta—or whoever is the final owner—in Pan Am, of American Express in Shearson Lehman, of the CELSA Group in Nueva Montaña Quijano or in its historical rival Torras Herrería y Construcciones, or so many other instances in which a healthy company takes over control of another seriously ill company with the purpose of restoring its health, produce a feeling of defeat in most of the managers in the company that has been taken over. Most of them were aware that there were problems and have fought hard to prolong the company's life. Sometimes, they admit that there is no other solution; they have no doubt in their minds that the company can only survive as part of another larger and stronger company, but this does not stop them from having a series of feelings such as sadness at having lost their independence, uncertainty as to the steps that the winner will take, doubts on their ability to function in the new context that will be created, the possible loss of status in the new organization chart that will be imposed, the impact of the failure on one's own image to suppliers, banks, customers, and even friends and relatives.

WINNERS AND LOSERS ARE NOT SO DIFFERENT

B oth sides come in for a surprise: neither are the winners supermen nor are the losers inept. It turns out that the winners do not have superpowers. To improve profitability, they cut down the workforce (simply reducing the denominator of the production/producers fraction); to match the supply to the demand, they put employees on short-time working or temporarily lay them off, thus reducing the number of hours worked. To reduce the debt, they increase the capital. They reduce expenses by means of austerity plans. Their management systems are completely normal and standard. On the other hand, they discover that the losers can come into work at 8 in the morning and leave at 10 at night, they too have their industrial knacks, they have some loyal customers due to the quality of the service they have been giving for many years, they are technically qualified, they have a good database for controlling their company. Sometimes, the winners wonder how could such good guys have got into such a fix. The problems are sometimes to be found in another sphere: the company was too small to compete in its sector, it erred in its market strategy, it borrowed too much, it did not reduce personnel in time, or, as we have seen, combinations of all this. But such things are not attributable to 99 per cent of the losers because they have no power of decision over them.

Case Study

A medium-sized building contractor reached an agreement to take over a real estate developer that owed it a lot of money and was in serious difficulties. The contractor had a diversified portfolio of building work, including civil work, dwellings, industrial construction and restoration. The developer had concentrated its activity in a coastal area with excess supply. The developer's portfolio was not bad but its financial situation was desperate. An injection of funds in the developer could be very profitable. Shortly after taking over the developer and while it was trying to put some order in the sales, building work in progress and building work that had been stopped, the winners were able to obtain a clear insight into the worth and experience of the developer's financial director. During his company's dying months, that man had worked miracles.

His knowledge of the local banks, of the instruments available and the quality of his personal relationships with creditors and investors were far above that of the building contractor's financial staff. Consequently, he was immediately given a prominent post in the turnaround team and in the future of the group of companies that came out of the takeover.

One can be sure with almost complete certainty that even the most problem-ridden company has able people who can attain excellent results if properly managed. Some of these people even discover the source of the problems afflicting them and are looking for a change of direction. The advantage of the existence of good people in the organization to be turned around is, among other things, their knowledge of the business in which the business unit to be reorganized operates. By integrating such people in the turnaround team, it is possible to progress much more quickly.

Some executives who have managed to successfully turn around companies or divisions acknowledge that the quality of the managers they found in the units to be restructured and which they recruited to the turnaround team did not match their position in the original organization chart. Thus, for example, a plant manager was a much better manager than his superior, the production manager. Consequently, when examining the management team of a unit to be restructured in order to determine who should be given the key responsibilities in the process, it is wise to consider the people in the top two or three levels on the basis of their personal features and not necessarily on the position they hold in the ailing unit's organization chart.

THE WINNERS ARE NOT TO BLAME

T he winners may implement measures that seem unfair to the losers. A team of researchers had been asked to make an almost superhuman effort to try to get a product ready for the market by a certain date. When the company was taken over by a new firm, the latter's managers concluded that it was not possible to get that product ready by that date and that it was not even important to put the product on the market at all; they cancelled the entire R&D project, assigned the researchers to other tasks and, in the case of employees on temporary contracts or hired as consultants, immediately terminated the contracts. When the case of a company requiring a turnaround is discussed in a management training programme inevitably a large part of the debate is centred on the dilemma of which parts go and which parts stay. Comfortably sitting in a business school classroom chair, some feel more surgical than others but all without exception eliminate, reassign, lay off, cancel and close.

Surprisingly enough, the people affected by the reorganizing procedure sometimes talk with respect and liking of the managers who were removed by the turnaround team, while they complain of the latter's lack of humanity and even of their incompetence in understanding the business. This is one of the less rewarding aspects of working in a corporate turnaround: to the overwhelming pressure of work and the uncertainty about the decisions that should be taken, one must add the lack of understanding shown by many people in the company and the erosion this may cause, particularly in the lower levels of the company if it reaches them.

But the bad guys are not the executives who are trying to put the company back on its feet. They did not create the problem. It was the negligence or mistaken judgements of the people who managed the company before the winners came that brought things to this pass. It is the managers who perhaps maintained the feather-bed atmosphere that everyone remembers as 'the good old days' who are responsible for the uncomfortable hardness of the turnaround period and one should make sure that most of the people working in the company know this.

THE PRESENTATION OF CREDENTIALS

This term—imported from the language of diplomacy—used to refer to the first contact between the winning management team and the losing management team. It is equally applicable to the entry in a company or business unit to be reorganized and to the purchase of a company. The first contact is extremely important and should take place as soon as the occasion presents itself. In the presentation, the winning team should introduce itself, explain its objectives and the general lines of action it proposes to follow. The presentation of credentials should be used to create an attitude of openness and resolute cooperation; it should be a declaration of 'starting afresh'.

There are cases when the managers of a company that is going to be reorganized do not know who the winners are, but follow in the press the course of the negotiations taking place at high level, or even outside of the company when the owners are not involved in the management. People know that there are other managers but as yet they are faceless. During these transitional periods, which may be lengthy, the company may suffer enormous losses: competent managers may choose to leave (taking with them, of course, mounds of information and ideas that would be useful for the company's recovery), and there is a generalized lassitude in the sales area, in employee affairs, in supplies. It is hard for people to fight when they do not know who they are fighting for.

When presenting credentials, it is important to avoid making too many promises. There is nothing worse than starting to promise things and not being able to keep them a couple of days later. Loquacious managers would be advised to write down what they are going to say at the presentation of credentials. When an executive receives the order from his superiors to make the presentation of credentials, he can be sure that that day he got out of bed on the wrong side. There is no doubt that it is a delicate task. There are very few concrete things that can be said and the executive would be wise to cross off on his own account a few of the things his superiors tell him to say, because he will be the one who will be remembered as saying that no one would lose their job, that plant X would not be closed, that the working conditions would be matched with plant Y, etc. Also, if it is not his superiors who put themselves on the line, it is easier for them not to feel fully committed to the initial promises if, as unfortunately happens, the situation of the company to be turned around goes from bad to worse.

The goal of the presentation of credentials should be to win the trust of the beaten managers, and to give the winning managers the image of being professional, honest people prepared to work very hard to save the dying unit (though if it is true that they are honest and diligent professionals, they will not have to try very hard to convey that image).

HOW TO TAKE POSSESSION

CASE STUDIES

When Fiat reached an agreement to enter Seat, in the early 1980s, and started to take joint charge of the company's management, it did not conceal its intention to eliminate the company's top managers. Not only did it make this known in certain places but also assigned its own executives, in parallel with Spanish executives, to the key functions. Thus, if some senior manager heard the rumour that he would soon be for the chop, so that he would have no doubts on the matter, an Italian would come to 'help' him carry out his responsibilities. The anti-Fiat reactions this generated were enormous, the unpopularity of the winning troops beat all records and, as Seat's top management still had its roots in the company's owner, INI, it is not surprising that Fiat's entry should fail. Many experts in the automobile industry are convinced that losing Seat was a serious strategic setback for Fiat. For INI, transferring Seat to Fiat at that time would no doubt have saved a lot of money. It is very likely that the failure of the operation was due to the lack of tact with which Fiat's turnaround team took possession.

A company operating in the household appliances industry took over another company that was generally considered as beyond hope. The managers responsible for restructuring and integrating the foundering unit started the project with a series of in-depth interviews with the members of the management team of the company to be taken over. Dividing them in functional groups of top managers, they asked them to explain the reasons for the decline and the projects and ideas they had for the future, subsequently discussing the subjects in greater depth in one-to-one meetings. A four-manager team from the winning company worked intensely in this initial contact phase. Some of these meetings were held during lunch or dinner so that the conversation could take place in a more relaxed atmosphere. After a few days, the turnaround managers met to adjust their reorganization plan. At that meeting, they exchanged opinions on the losing managers and a working organization chart was drawn up for the initial turnaround period. In this organization chart, which was very horizontal, two of the losing managers held top level posts. They reacted with enormous enthusiasm and the cooperation provided by the company was extraordinary.

Entry into a business unit to be reorganized is always easier if it is possible quickly to include some of the losing managers in the team that will lead the turnaround. In some cases, resounding successes have been achieved by integrating in the process prestigious managers who left the company when it was going downhill and whose recommendations were perhaps ignored by the senior management. The other managers, supervisors and workers view this integrative attitude as a sign of good intentions and of assigning priority to solving the problems, rather than to possible shadowy goals that the imagination of disappointed people might suggest.

Ambiguous organization charts are not a good way of entering an ailing unit. All companies have an appreciable dose of ambiguity in their organization. Even in such tightly geared companies as Ford or IBM, it is possible to find ambiguity. A gearwheel that did not have the slightest play would not turn, it would be fixed. However, the type of ambiguity is specific to each company, it is generated with time and the company's unique culture, and its limits are known only by those who have been in the company for some time. So, it is all very well to have organization charts that do not include lines that everyone knows are there, important meetings that are not on the agenda of the management committee, the control committee or the budgets committee, and reporting lines that bypass certain managers for certain things, etc. But when one overuses ambiguity in a unit which one has entered primarily to restructure, the end result can be considerable confusion. It is therefore advisable to make an effort to be concrete and explicit in the organization processes adopted in the units to be reorganized.

HOW TO HAND OVER TO THE WINNER

Case Study

The president and board of directors of a major business group had spent six months negotiating the purchase of a particular company. The candidate company was in a truly desperate situation and, judging from the amount of stockpiling it was doing, it was probably preparing a suspension of payments. The company's owners seemed to have handed over their shares to a renowned lawyer who, to all intents and purposes, appeared to be the company's owner. It was clear to the buying managers the other party wished to sell, that the company was a timebomb and that the lawyer could not spin out the sale indefinitely. However, they also knew that the ailing company, in spite of its desperate situation, had a strategic value due to its geographical location and market positioning and that the seller would try to get the highest price that these factors could command. Finally, an agreement was reached. Thereupon, the lawyer took out some contracts. 'I know we haven't mentioned this before,' he said, 'but a few years ago contracts were signed with some of the managers should the company change owner and they should be asked to leave.'

One did not need to be a FBI expert to tell that the contracts had been signed that very afternoon. The buying managers considered that the contracts were improper and, although they did not wish to break the agreement they had reached, they did feel that the contracts should be renegotiated. One thing that was clear in their minds was that their future plans would definitely not include any of the people 'protected' by the contracts.

It is a common occurrence in high-risk situations when a company's management is changing hands that some of its managers obtain contracts that guarantee large payments should they be discontinued in the company. When a management team enters a business to turn it around, they do not feel particularly motivated to use the very limited cash available to pay off the people who caused the cataclysm. Also, anyone who turns up with a protective contract automatically identifies himself as someone who prefers to collect his money and go. Sometimes, to avoid further problems, the incoming managers pay and are left with the thought that they should not have done so. In most cases, the incoming managers negotiate with the beneficiaries of the contracts and finally give them a fraction of what they ask. In other cases, the incoming managers simply refuse to honour such contracts and let the courts decide the matter.

Whether or not to protect oneself with a contract* is a dilemma that must be decided by all managers in a decaying company in danger of being boarded by a turnaround team. If the manager has any chance of joining the winning team, the existence of such a contract will almost definitely ensure that this does not happen. A protective contract is a poor safe-conduct to give to the winners.

We said at the beginning of this chapter that the winners do not have superpowers. This is something that offers enormous opportunities to the losers. An executive in a company boarded by a turnaround team would be wise to show an open and cooperative attitude, be receptive to new ideas and be prepared to cooperate enthusiastically with the new leadership. However, he should also use all his skill to make his abilities and how he uses them in the daily performance of his duties known. There are managers who habitually protect their plot by limiting the upwards, downwards and sideways flow of information on their work. The secretive executive will be in for a hard time with a turnaround team. They do not like to see beaten executives withholding information and it is one of the main causes of extremely summary trials and expeditive actions. The best armour an executive in the losing company has is his *savoir-faire* should he be able to place it at the unconditional service of a winning executive.

CONCLUSION

In the relationship between winners and losers, the ideal situation is that in which there are no winners or losers. The losers must take up the winners' ideology and the winners must accept that they can learn something from the losers. Both parties must make the company's health their priority, staking, if necessary, possible short-term personal satisfactions. Politics, intriguing, sabotaging the newcomers and corrosive attitudes to

---

* These contracts are usually called golden parachutes. As we have seen, more than one executive's parachute has failed to open and the more gold it has, the more it weighs.

lower management levels must be avoided. Past structures and reporting relationships must be abolished when they have been ruled out by the turnaround managers. The people in the ailing business unit must display maximum flexibility as the outsiders will come on board with a relatively rigid turnaround plan.

7

The facilitators

I n chemistry, they are called catalysts, substances that speed up a chemical reaction. When implementing a business strategy, investing by the purchase of or disinvesting by the sale of companies, in large-scale mergers, in winning large orders, in negotations with the national or supranational government (the EC, for example), in the creation of consortia or groupings of companies to undertake or defend certain objectives and—why not?—in the subject of this book, corporate turnarounds, of which all the above may form part, there usually appear people or institutions who play the role of facilitators, assisting the process in some manner.

In chemistry, a poor catalyst or a catalyst in bad condition can 'poison' a reaction and even stop production for several days, causing substantial losses. Likewise, in business processes, a poor facilitator may also poison a process by making it not viable or increasing its cost.

Chemical catalysts are generous substances as they cheapen the processes that take place in the reactors without consuming themselves. In actual fact, they stand a little to one side of the reaction. The facilitators in the business world usually have a less altruistic objective and seek to enrich themselves—either by increased wealth or increased power—and to come out strengthened in some way from the processes they facilitate. It is true that there are some facilitators who genuinely seek professional success from the processes they stimulate, remaining like their chemical counterparts discretely in the background, but they are a distinct minority.

However, the fact is that facilitators exist and rarely can one do without their involvement in corporate turnaround processes. They form part of that which McCormack* would include in 'what they do not teach you in the Harvard Business School'. The rest of the chapter will be devoted to these facilitators. Many turnaround experts, as we shall see, recommend their selective use.

FACILITATOR-CONSULTANTS

CASE STUDIES

McNulty Bangor Group International, the renowned consultancy, had managed to get into Dauradella Betas y Fils, a very strong firm belonging to Josep Dauradella, the well-known Catalan entrepreneur who had created from nothing (and that really is creating) an empire of textile, fashion, franchised distribution, finance, transport, etc., companies. After years of continued growth in sales and profits, Dauradella Betas y Fils had started to falter and some of Dauradella's closest managers had advised him to call in a major consultancy to help him get out of the rut. Carlos Palau was the vice-president† who was assigned responsibility for the account. Surprisingly, even to Carlos, Mr Dauradella was very enthusiastic about the consultancy. Although his character had been forged in the hard world of buying and selling,

---

* McCormack wrote the book *What They Don't Teach You at Harvard Business School*. McCormack is one of those authors who exploits the name of Harvard, which always sells. Most of the things he explains are learnt in Harvard. Harvard is a school where one learns, not where one is taught.

†International consultants have a career scale which goes something like this: associate, senior associate, vice-president, senior vice-president, president. The higher one gets, the more one earns. By keeping the pyramid with a wide base—many associates and few vice-presidents—the latter can command very high incomes.

he had an exceptional natural intelligence and he enjoyed the challenge of strategic logic. The fact that the warehouse in the Ronda de San Pedro, which was always full of streetsellers, some of them gypsies, and which he affectionately called 'The Fleamarket', was now a strategic business unit—SBU$_3$ to be precise—he found very exciting. The fact that to that scoundrel Martí who had left him—he who owed everything he knew to Dauradella—to start up on his own, he could do what he would have called 'dirty tricks' but which were now 'entry barriers' seemed to him to be exquisite good taste.

Palau and Dauradella got on well. Not anyone could speak with Dauradella. He would take the telephone if it was the president of the Banco Central or of the Generalitat, but not if it was the Banco Central's regional manager or a head of department in the Generalitat. But, miraculously enough, Palau had unlimited access to Dauradella's time. Dauradella's closest employees began to feel a bit bothered about this sudden affair between their boss and the consultant. When McNulty Bangor Group International presented their report, the organization chart proposed for Dauradella Betas y Fils included a position to be created alongside Dauradella with a profile very similar to that of Carlos Palau. Other consultants in the renowned multinational had followed the example. Dauradella Betas y Fils had a lot of money. There, it was possible to make the jump from consultant (a kind of intellectual brothel that sells its knowledge by the hour) to executive (which was like being bound in legal matrimony to the company), going straight up the ladder to the top and with a good salary. What was more, the senior executives in Dauradella Betas y Fils were people who had been with Dauradella in the difficult times during the creation and rapid growth of the company, who had worked shoulder to shoulder with him, day and night, Saturdays and Sundays, but none of them had a master's degree and none of them knew who Michael Porter* was.

In his romance with Dauradella, Carlos Palau had gone beyond the functions corresponding to a strategy consultant and proposed new business deals, for which he offered to provide contacts obtained from other consultancy assignments carried out for his company, probably thinking that the transgression of the ethical frontier would be offset by the virtuous practice of his present loyalty (which after all is a value).

One day, the intuitive Dauradella sensed the subterranean current of discontent that was growing in his company and, one by one, sounded out his right-hand men. They did not have the brilliant strategic logic of Carlos and Michael Porter but was loyalty and years of steady effort, a very valuable asset. If he had taken the step—and the idea had occurred to him—of taking on Carlos Palau as his vice-president, the uproar would have been enormous. As time went by, he began to feel increasingly uncomfortable with himself. Carlos and his bunch were doing a good job but they were going too fast. Dauradella simply put them back where they belonged: as consultants. Later, Dauradella confessed that the recoil produced by the situation had prevented some of the ideas contributed by the consultants from being implemented. In short. Dauradella himself acknowledged that his lack of skill in handling the relationship with the consultants put back almost a year the commencement of the process to get the company going again.

Three employers had agreed to purchase a company with the aim of closing it, as there was too much

---

* Michael Porter is a Harvard Business School professor who has achieved a well-earned fame for his ideas on competitive strategy. He is also one of the highest paid consultants in the world.

production on the market and the company's production facilities were in a pretty bad shape after years of little and ill-judged investment. They thought that the company could be bought relatively cheaply as its owner was an elderly man without any direct heirs. Besides, because of the excess supply, there would be little point in investing to turn around the company. By selling out, thought the three employers, their competitor would be offloading a bothersome problem. Although they had no doubts that closing could be a good solution, they were not so clear about how to approach this closure. Closing was necessary, they thought, for the good of their own companies.

If they created a kind of consortium to close the factory, this might not be interpreted very favourably by the unions: 'Three powerful employers join forces to deprive hundreds of families of their livelihood.' The conclusion would be that closing would cost a lot of money and they would probably have to make additional concessions to the workforces in their own companies.

One of them proposed to take responsibility for the closure. He was prepared to be the one who bought the company and managed the closure. Of course, the other two would share the cost of the purchase with him and would pay, let us say, a fee for seeing through the closure operation. This fee would include what the 'closing' employer estimated would be the cost of the managers he would have to employ plus the outside advisers (labour relations experts, legal advisers, etc.). The other two were not sure about this alternative. Perhaps he would not be able to complete the job and would leave the operation unfinished or, in the worst case, unfinishable. Perhaps they thought that once inside the company to be closed, the market conditions could change and, instead of closing, he would opt for restructuring and strengthening it. One of them said that one of his directors had mentioned the name of a bureau that specialized in this sort of thing. They agreed to pay a visit to the bureau.

Housed in an apartment in the centre of Madrid, well-decorated but without giving the impression of having excessive overheads, the bureau was run by three professionals in their 50s. Wearing striped shirts, the occasional white collar, with a cheery manner and a general style drawn from the McKinsey boys, two of the associates asked questions about the problem. They were short and progressive questions, aimed at getting into the matter without showing too much general or specific ignorance. One did not have to be Sherlock Holmes to realize that they had never closed a company and had never worked in that industry.

After nibbling at the problem for a while, they started to understand what was involved and provided examples—as closely related to the situation as they could—of things they had done (or so they hoped) to create an image of experience and professionalism. They obviously wanted to get the assignment. Their interest in the assignment led them to offer guarantees without explaining how they would go about it, which obviously was what the employers were most interested in: how would they do it? how would they close it? how long would they take to close it? and if the workers decide they don't like it and occupy the factory?

No sooner had they stepped out of the door, the three employers knew at least one thing for sure: they had wasted their time. They had told the associates that they would think it over and would call them back. One was chosen to made the call and all three would look for another alternative.

Another of the employers suggested that one of the big multinational consulting firms could perhaps help them. He had recently been a customer of one of these firms and so he was detailed to explore the possibility.

The answer was: 'We cannot take direct responsibility for closing but we can design a highly detailed closing process which could be implemented by one of your teams, who would only have to follow our instructions step by step.'

The employers pictured themselves in a situation with furious workers raising barricades in a certain town while frontmen were clinging to the telephone, with a 'closure PERT' in their hands, desperately asking the consultants for solutions. Obviously that did not fit the bill either.

Both in the case of the associates and in that of the multinational consultants, we are talking about multi-thousand pound fees. These we could estimate at about £100,000 to £150,000 per month (in 1987).

CASE STUDY

This example is about a prestigious lawyer. He has managed to get himself invited to lunch by an employer. Through the friend of a friend, he has conveyed to the employer the message that he 'can facilitate' such-and-such an operation which he has learned the employer is interested in in order to complete a repositioning and consolidation strategy in a certain sector. He defines himself as a personal friend of Mr X's, who is one of the key people in the operation, and as personal lawyer to the financier Y, who may be crucial for orchestrating it. 'I never lie,' he often says but at a certain moment, he says, 'I can tell X something that will mislead him and make him go where we want him to.' (An important ethical nuance for anyone looking for a subject for a PhD thesis in this field: deceiving is not ethical, but inducing someone to deceive themselves is.) He provides frequent examples of his close relations with X and Y to persuade the employer to put the operation in his hands. He uses the well-known reluctant virgin approach for his soft-selling*: 'I have nothing to gain from this but I thought that you were interested . . . if I can do you a favour . . .' The lawyer was a master in the art and obviously, the employer acceded. Whether or not the operation was done is another matter. It could be that the prestigious lawyer neither knew X nor that he was personal lawyer to Y but that he had certain possibilities of approaching both, particularly if he introduced himself as the employer's representative. It may even be that getting the assignment from the employer gave him the argument he needed to try to approach X and Y. It could be that the employer was a master in discerning questions and that it was clear that the lawyer was taking him for a ride. It could even have happened that the prestigious lawyer managed to orchestrate the operation, in which case his bill could have reached six figures and it could even be that it was a fair price. However, the lawyer failed in his attempt and said nothing more. The employer then called financier Y himself and, to his surprise, he got on to the phone immediately. Consequently, this was a case of a 'redundant' turnaround catalyst.

This sideways manner of advancing is very typical of some facilitators. They are friends with everyone, know about everything that is going on, get into businesses and, if they can, sit down and stay there. With their crab-like gait, they manage to filter themselves through the cracks of operations in progress or prospective deals. With their prestige, their power, their friends, many do not dare to ask, 'But who invited you to this party?' Some think, 'If he's interested in it, I'd rather he play with me.'

---

* These are terms used internationally to define certain approaches. Reluctant virgin means that a maiden who has doubts as to whether she should cease to be one becomes much more attractive to her suitor, precisely because of this vacillating attitude. Soft selling means unaggressive selling, creating the conditions for the buyer to take the initiative.

CASE STUDY

The company had accumulated an enormous debt with the Social Security. The team of consultants claimed to be able to do the impossible in this field—infinite deferrals, scaled payments which meant paying a little today and a little bit more tomorrow, token interest. If the matter was put in their hands, with their top level contacts, not even the administrative director himself would recognize the company's real balance sheet. The company had simply not paid the Social Security contributions although it had recorded and acknowledged every penny of its debt in the books. They knew that something could be got by negotiating with the Social Security but they were not sure how much. To not do anything had been their way of deceiving themselves. But the situation could not be continued any longer, the Social Security had sent them an ultimatum.

In the end, the consultants got everything that could be got within the law for which, obviously, it was not necessary to speak with the corresponding minister. It was not a bad result. The company's management closely monitored the consultants' steps and did not see the exercise of any superpowers at any time. As a result, they finally reached the conclusion that what the consultants gave them they could have got equally well on their own and they felt that they had been taken for a ride. They had been taken for a ride because the consultants had not used their superpowers in the operation to erase debts with the state. They had got what the law says can be got, and some promise from some friend that 'we'll see later' but nothing on paper.

Some consultants create an aura of having superpowers, or that they might have them if the stars are in the right conjunctions. The employer in a fix likes to believe in superpowers. They give him the possibility of deceiving himself for a few days more.

125

When the consultant does not use his superpowers, the employer in a fix thinks, 'What's he waiting for to eat his spinach? Doesn't he realize that the affair's loaded with kryptonite?' Then, when it is clear that the consultant does not have nor ever will have superpowers, the employer in a fix gets mad and may even put all consultants in the same boat of hoaxers.

A colleague explained to me that once someone came to him with a similar type of problem. He urgently needed a consultant with superpowers. He put him in contact with an ex-minister whom he had been assured could fly. Some time later, he received a case of Moët et Chandon from that someone, leaving him with the thought that that ex-minister could in fact fly.

During the 1980s, to help strengthen the country's companies, subsidies and aid programmes have been granted in Spain for all sorts of reasons: job creation, location in Zones of Urgent Reindustrialization (ZUR), research and development, industrial reorganization, aids for export, etc. In many of these programmes, any company that fulfilled the requirements received its subsidy. But for most employers, receiving money free from the state always comes as a surprise and this creates the opportunity to apply for grants and subsidies in exchange for a commission. In some cases, it is even possible to get a 'fixed' fee and a commission as there are employers who can be fooled better with a fixed fee and a variable fee than with a fixed fee only or with a variable fee only. Some people like it elaborate.

If 10 per cent of the grants and subsidies have been 'managed' and the variable fee has been 10 per cent, then 1 per cent of the budget has gone to the agents. This calculation, which has no real basis and is only intended to gauge orders of magnitude, would give management fees—in this case it is not so exaggerated—amounting to tens of millions of pounds. In many cases, the agents have done absolutely nothing. The grant or subsidy would have been given anyway. In other cases, the agent may have managed to 'order the pile' of papers on the desk of some friend or partner in the administration, while at the same time helping to redress the unfair way the state treats its employees.

This type of consultancy, which is to be found in all the capitals of Spain (central or regional) and—of course!—in

Brussels and Washington,* is usually practised particularly by ex-government officials who 'know the ropes' and 'know how to get around in there'. Sometimes, they define themselves as lobbyists. Although it is usual that in particular the senior officials get to where they are by a very different route— socialists, labourists, communists, christian democrats, greens, nationalists, conservatives, etc.—when they decide to practise lobbying, they usually lose the 'vocational' prejudice and are able to negotiate from a completely neutral stance. Sometimes, the more 'vocational' one has been, the more 'neutral' one can be later on. The same thing happens to people who leave a religious order.

THE PRESS AND PUBLIC RELATIONS

T hings may not be going well for the company and its problems are starting to get talked about. Some banks were asking the typical questions that someone asks when they can imagine the answer but want to check that you are lying to them. In any case, others are worse off and there is a good chance of being able to weather the storm. Then a director has the idea of using 'public relations'. How should the matter be approached? Should the company contract a public relations company? Should it simply contract a journalist? Should one of the senior managers be made responsible for it? Would it be enough to send a nice Christmas present to a few well-known journalists? Would it be better to hold a board meeting in Las Palmas de Gran Canaria and then invite some reporters with their wives or girlfriends there for a press conference? Finally, it is decided to contact a journalist who, while still working for a certain newspaper, works overtime, giving private classes to a few customers. He could 'influence' some of his colleagues, 'share' some information, 'attract' the attention with some article of his on some positive aspect of the company that needed to be brought out, 'screen' certain colleagues by telling the

---

* Since 1990 and particularly in 1991, it has become apparent that in Tokyo too there seems to be a certain know-how in taking short-cuts by paying tolls.

127

company beforehand who it could trust and who not. One never knows, there are always those naive-looking people who smile gratefully when you give them the news item, nod their head, understand your point of view and then bring out something highly incendiary which contains only part of what you have told them.

Obviously, the public relations 'industry' has a right to exist: it keeps a certain number of people out of the dole queue. One journalist explained to me that a certain computer company whose president liked to appear in the press sent so many press releases* each day that one colleague said that he would paper the walls with them. I asked him if those press releases were effective, to which he answered, 'Not with us, but there are so many business publications that someone will publish them.' Journalists who have been bought by a company are readily spotted by their colleagues and are not popular.

Some public relations have destroyed more than one company or business. Using public relations as part of a negotiating strategy or any other type of action is extremely hazardous. However, the board meetings are full of opinions to the effect of 'we should use the press for this'. There are public relations companies that offer a fixed remuneration and a success fee† if they get results, which implies that they undertake to 'create opinion' in one direction or another.

Public relations people have been known to offer their services to 'create opinion' in favour of a certain project or deal among specific people or institutions: 'I'm sure you realize that, like everywhere else, you've got to pay the toll.' One must be very careful about paying the toll. Unfortunately, there are

---

* The press release is usually a communiqué containing a certain excess of redundant information on a favourable subject. Press releases are usually sent on the assumption that journalists are stupid and are written in such a manner that even though one cuts it in half or misses out a line, it still conveys the desired information. Even so, some journalists manage to transcribe it so that it says the opposite of what is intended.

† Success fee is the term used by head hunters, those who buy and sell companies, or who in general can achieve a result whose economic worth is completely unrelated with the time spent in achieving it.

specialists in privatizing public information flows and turning themselves into collectors on these communication routes.

In recent years, communication and image consultancies have proliferated all over the world and also in Spain. Some are already multinationals within their profession, with branches in all the world's major capitals. Some of these companies and the people who work in them are excellent professionals. The impact of news in the modern world is enormous. At a frivolous dinner, a group of four friends could invent an absurd news item; if one of them were to be able to get it published in *El Pais* on the next day, the reader can be sure that at least one of the others would think, 'Well, just look at that, we thought it was a joke and it was true.' If the same news were to be published in *The Financial Times*, the consequences could be unimaginable.

Table 7.1 *Some of the functions of the communication and image companies*

- Analytic compilation of everything that has been published in the press on the project
- Deduction of competitor information strategies
- Deduction of more sensitive information areas
- Knowledge of the media world and its influence
- Access to the various media
- Updating in subjects related with the culture of a situation or country (what should or should not be done)
- Effective communication of specific information
- Identify how a company or project is perceived and alter that perception

---

In a climate, such as in Europe and probably more so in Spain, where there is a lot of press and strong competition, the news stories are not seriously screened, journalists have neither the resources nor the time to check out their information, and sometimes all sorts of things get published. In the press, there are always people who can be manipulated, some because of sheer lack of professionalism and others—perhaps the minority—because of a lack of ethics (if the former does not imply the latter). There are also excellent professionals but, unfortunately, the least presentable are usually the most well-known to employers, in some cases out of fear. If one combines the impact of news, the great volume of media and the press's lack of resources, one comes to the conclusion that it makes financial sense to be able to count on the advice of a good communication and image company. If one wishes to implement large-scale projects in a foreign country, to be advised by good professionals familiar with the area which the project is going to affect may be fundamental for facilitating its progress. However, the communication and image company must stay within its field and not venture into project design or implementation phases outside its area of competence (Table 7.1). In Europe, in order to obtain regular dedication to a medium-sized company (£300–600 million in annual sales), a good communication and image company may represent an annual cost between £30,000 and £60,000, plus expenses (travel, advertising, etc.), if the situations are normal and there is no permanent confrontation with other companies, the state or the public.

CORROSIVE CATALYSTS

Facilitators do not act in isolation. Just as in the jungle there are levels of action that are respected: the chief lion chooses the prey, hunts it and eats what he likes best, then come the other lions in the group, then the hyenas and jackals, then the vultures, etc. The same thing happens with a company or business project. It may happen that if the public relations guy sees that the matter may slip through his fingers if he tries to go it alone, he approaches the prestigious lawyer who immediately comes to his support. If they see that they are going to lose it anyway, they may call in the consultant. 'I scratch your back, you scratch my back.' A certain sales operation concerning a Madrid building fell through because there were so many 'interested parties' that the final price was way above the market price.

When some employers who have bought companies in Spain in recent years have looked a little bit deeper, they have found the endearing image of the sow feeding a litter of piglets, which included lawyers, congressmen, wives of union leaders, journalists, ex-union men and all manner of advisers. More than one sow would have become pure skin and bones after feeding so many piglets. Many have wondered to what extent the deterioration of some of these companies may not be due to having so many advisers on board.

Facilitators operate in special culture mediums. As Allen of the MIT* would say in his study of information flows, facilitators place themselves where there are information flows or create their own information flows. Thus, in Madrid, for example, a facilitator always has lunch with some prey in a luxury restaurant (£50 per person on average in 1989) and may attend in the evening or night some selective event organized by the business press (election of the most entrepreneurial entrepreneur of the year, for example) or to a socioeconomic debate. The facilitators themselves organize frequent receptions to which government officials, employers, senior executives and other facilitators allow themselves to be invited without too much demur. Often, there are facilitators that arrive at 11 p.m. and leave at 12 midnight and others that arrive at 12 midnight and leave at 2 a.m. In such cases, it is highly likely that the facilitator has been at two receptions during the same night. The situation is very similar in other cities in the West and East.

The goal is to get image recognition: 'I'll ring you tomorrow'; reminder: 'We must look at that subject again, now's the time'; field research:† 'Do you know anything about that new credit to Argentina?'; fishing: 'We must do something together, it would be great to work with you'; hypothesis contrasting: 'I've heard

---

* Thomas Allen has found that companies well connected to a good infrastructure of information flows (journals, congresses, universities, consultants) are much more innovative than those that keep themselves relatively closed.

† Field research is the data obtained by interview in order to gain greater insight into a problem. As a friend of mine says, 'When a facilitator does field work, don't let him catch you with your garden hat on.'

that Tom's leaving the Ministry'; more fishing: 'Yes, and it seems that he will be replaced by Robert, who's a good friend of mine.' Turnarounds, with their sharp edges rubbing against so many stakeholders, are fertile ground for offering all manner of opportunities to influence. Some of these influences may be harmful and even corrosive.

CONCLUSION

These days, virtually no one can go it alone in big business. With the multitude of variables that must be processed and the large number of stakeholders, very few entrepreneurs can successfully work in this field without help. Sometimes, the communications media place so much emphasis on the virtues of the leader that his assistants become shadowy forms in the background, but they are always there. The main feature that defines a great businessman—or woman—is, as we have already said, his or her ability to choose and retain a high-quality team of assistants. Failure and corporate decline often correlate with the lack of this ability.

Among the assistants that must be attracted, retained and motivated, there are obviously the facilitators, although, as we have seen, sometimes one must not try too hard to attract them. Working with facilitators is more difficult than working with executives because there is no permanent link, there is virtually no hierarchical relationship and they resist control. However, there are some things that only they can do and one must know how to use them.

1. One must proceed with great care when buying a facilitator's services. As with everything, there are specialists and specialists must be able to show a record of successful assignments. If we are going to undergo open heart surgery, a recent graduate from the best teaching clinic in the United States is better than nothing but a surgeon who has operated on 500 similar cases with a 98 per cent success rate is even better. With a little bit of research, one can find these things out. We've got a lot at stake.

2. One must separate roles. A strategy consultant should not act as a business broker because, even without wanting to, he may end up involving us in the businesses he has in his portfolio. A legal adviser should not advise us on a certain strategy—we are going to try a hostile takeover on such-and-such a company, for example—because we have not contracted him to advise us on strategy but so that he may legally optimize the agreements we have obtained in the implementation of our own strategy. A financial agent should not push us into a deal he considers to be good and for which he provides all the money required because we may end up to our ears in debt, working for him and without really knowing why.

3. We should assess the possibilities of acting on our own without intermediaries. Many people have the idea of an inaccessible administration or inaccessible giant corporations. This image is increasingly less true. Unfortunately, the administration is so big and so heavy that there are still enough bureaucrats for everyone. They are dying for you to go and see them. They too need to go and eat in fashionable restaurants. Without companies and employers, they cannot do their work. In Brussels, for example, it is even easier. The EC bureaucracy must be the largest coffee consumer in the world and officials working in the multitude of little cubicles along the maze of corridors are dying to offer cups of coffee to anyone who will help them to deceive themselves as to the usefulness of their well-paid semi-employment. The world's great businessmen do business because people with opportunities walk into their offices. They cannot shut themselves up in an ivory tower because then they would not do any business. They are often waiting for that decisive telephone call and they know better than anyone that if the business comes direct, it is better business than if one has to pay an intermediary.

4. One must think that for a minority of people, in some moment of weakness or repentance, ethics may become important. To see how an ex-colleague uses information

obtained when he worked in the administration to sell his services may close doors. Excessive inbreeding* may be suspicious. To what extent is it true that a facilitator is retained to prevent all our secrets flowing to our direct competitors? It is usually a good guarantee of ethical behaviour that a facilitator maintains contact with only one company in a particular industry and does not accept assignments from a company if he has worked for another company in the same industry in the recent past. The relationship between remuneration and results should be balanced and perceived to be so by the members of the team taking part in the project. When those who stake their livelihood in a complicated project see an outside facilitator, who only plays to win, walk off with a fat envelope, they become frustrated and the resulting discontent may lead to a general demand for similar compensation levels, a lack of cooperation in the project and the possible destruction of the human team. Laws exist and breaking them may have consequences several years later. Sometimes, a group of people, even the government itself, may be prepared to turn a blind eye to a certain shoddy piece of work because the facilitator so-and-so, who knows everyone, who is everyone's friend, asks it as a special favour and even offers a procedure 'similar to that which was used in such-and-such a case, which everyone remembers'. But watch out for that guy who is in the second or third row, who today is a nobody but tomorrow may be wielding the stick and decides to reopen the file.

5. It should be remembered that if the virtue of discretion is an exceedingly important quality in any person and for any thing, in companies and business discretion is vital. When a facilitator uses concrete examples, with names and dates, to

---

* In business terms, inbreeding refers to excessive in-house promotion. In services, it means working for the same customers. The opposite to this is 'cross-fertilization', which is associated with the enriching contribution of people outside the company (new blood) with original ideas. In services, it means having a diversified customer portfolio.

prove his experience; when he confides secrets, frequently using expressions such as 'between you and me . . .', 'don't tell anyone else but . . .', 'just between the two of us . . .', etc, and then proceeds to recount situations that are relevant or irrelevant to the case but which violate the privacy of other people or companies, then it would be logical to suppose that, at some time or another, our own confidential data will be laid out on the table.

6. One must always remember that the management of time is a highly important skill in business activity. Everything needs time. One must know when to move fast and when to move slow. One must not spend more time on things than is strictly necessary. The facilitator tends to expand time. The good entrepreneur tends to compress it. However, compressing does not mean deciding quickly. A facilitator should never be hired on impulse. The matter must be thought over seriously with close subordinates, partners or trustworthy board directors. All of us go through life carrying a stage and some sets. Wherever we decide to stop, we put up the stage, choose the set that most suits the occasion and raise the curtain. Facilitators are master choreographers and can easily outact the best actor. So, one must listen to them, let them speak, remain silent as much as possible, and finally tell them that we will think it over and, as tomorrow we have to fly to Frankfurt (a place that always goes down well), we will give them a decision by Monday without fail. During that period, which includes a weekend, we separate out in our mind the tenor from the choreography and finally, we take away even the orchestra. That way, we can see whether or not there is really something there to offer.

7. One should do something so that our children can live in a world that is cleaner, more constructive, more oriented towards creating wealth than dissipating it. We should distinguish between that which adds value and that which adds nothing. That which adds value has a price and it is fair to pay it even though that price may be high. What does not

add value not only should not be paid for but one should also have the courage to clearly say that we give no value to it. The design of a strategy, the identification of an opportunity, the contribution of an argument for a difficult negotiation, the achievement of a complex business result (a large order, a difficult collection, a loan in good conditions, a solid labour agreement, etc.) are things that add value. Telling you someone else's secrets, introducing you to a friend, getting you into a ministry, telling you who the president or vice-president of the government likes or does not like, finding out for you the current status of affair X which is being handled by lawyer Y or official Z—it is by no means so clear whether these things add value and, often, are a sign of poor ethics.

8. One should remember that facilitators may be extremely useful when they contribute intelligence, experience and professionalism: when they act in their place, doing what they have been hired to do, coordinating their actions with the rest of the company's management team, when their work is as transparent as is possible in the institutional environment within which they operate, when they have won a name for themselves and a reputation for competence and ethical behaviour, and when they know how to find a suitable balance between the value they add and the part of that value they take as remuneration. Besides, professional facilitators are a variable cost, which is another advantage.

8

The contribution of science

A lot has been written about the subject of corporate turnaround while research has lagged a little way behind. It is a highly complex problem in which a great many variables are involved. Nobody expects it to be possible to conceive a generic mathematical model which includes all the variables and enables concrete solutions to be obtained for specific problems. Sometimes, little bits of the problem have been isolated for the purpose of studying them separately to find formal ways of accounting for reality or predicting possible results of certain actions. Such attempts have not been very successful. On other occasions, the problem has been approached from a more general angle, perhaps placing more emphasis on some aspect and trying to synthesize certain structures. This type of approach is much more useful for understanding the problems of corporate turnaround and for helping the people who intend to face such a task.

The general approaches are often based on the analysis of a certain inventory of real-life situations. We will refer to some interesting contributions by authors who have directly or indirectly tackled the problem we are studying here. It is not in the least our intention to be exhaustive. We could probably include in this analysis of the literature such classics as Alfred Sloan's book *My Years in General Motors* as it explains decisions that brought about a profound change in the company's orientation and allowed it to achieve an industrial leadership that was maintained for many years. However, we would prefer to concentrate on recent works, which approach the turnaround problem within the current international climate in which our companies are competing.

TURNAROUND CASE STUDIES

The first category comprises case studies describing turnaround situations. There are a large number of case studies produced by professors in business management schools which can be obtained through these institutions' teaching material distribution services. Leading schools in producing material in this field are the Harvard Business School in Boston, the IMD in Lausanne, and the IESE in Barcelona.

Also, a large number of books have been published describing specific turnaround situations or a series of such situations. For example, the president of Scandinavian Airlines, Jan Carlzon, is the author of the 1987 best-seller entitled *Moments of Truth*. In this book, Mr Carlzon tells us how he turned around Scandinavian Airline's (SAS) subsidiaries Vingresor and Linjeflyg and, later, how he turned around SAS itself. In 1980, after 17 years in the black, SAS was going to declare a loss of $20 million. The study of the history of air transport companies shows that turnaround efforts almost always start with selling off part of the aircraft fleet. Jan Carlzon never considered this solution. At that time, Europe was in the throes of a deep recession that was also hitting the airlines very hard and SAS had already made a generalized cost reduction effort.

Jan Carlzon decided to focus the company on a type of customer who had to carry on flying even during times of recession: the business executive. He created what he called the 'EuroClass' to give a highly improved service to full-fare passengers and also launched 147 projects to raise the quality of service offered by SAS. These projects included an ambitious training plan for more than half of the company's 20,000 employees and a plan for increasing flight punctuality. After taking almost one year to develop, this plan was implemented with $45 million in capital investment and $12 million in extra operating expenses. However, the company's new 'focus' enabled it to reduce costs in other expense items to give a net outlay of $40 million. Jan Carlzon made enormous efforts to create an awareness among all his employees and to motivate them to contribute personally to the turnaround effort. Many experts consider that Jan Carlzon achieved an extraordinary leadership effect and was able to bring about a dramatic change in the attitude of SAS's personnel during those years.

The goal of Carlzon's plan was to increase profits by $25 million in the first year, $40 million in the second year and $50 million in the third year. The result actually achieved was an improvement of $80 million dollars in the first year. The number of full-fare passengers increased by 23 per cent over the three-year period and the number of passengers on economy fares increased by 7 per cent. All this was achieved in an economic climate, in 1982, in which the international airlines as a whole sustained losses of $2 billion. In 1983, *Fortune* voted SAS as the best airline company for the business executive.

In his book, Jan Carlzon explains his own experience of this process and what he considers to be crucial in obtaining the results that were achieved. He himself perceives his alternative as a flight forward, as defined in this book, and gives the example of a Swedish folktale in which the hero jumps across a deep crevice to reach his goal. The strategy chosen by Carlzon was obviously successful but he perceives his success in his ability to implement it. His main tool was perhaps his extraordinary communication skills. Jan Carlzon makes superb use of any opportunity to reach his personnel, even through his interviews in the press. His main concern seems to be to get the front-line person, the person who is giving the service and is in contact with the customer, to increase his or her qualitative and quantitative performance through a greater motivation. In 1991, SAS started to have problems again and it seems that the idyll between the company's top management and, at least, part of its personnel and very particularly the pilots, has cooled off, but, as we have already said previously, the merit of a turnaround process is no less because some years later new problems appear. Whether we like it or not, corporate life is a dynamic process.

On similar lines to Carlzon's book is that written by John Harvey-Jones (in 1988), who was chairman of ICI and who also managed significantly to revitalize his company in the early 1980s. Harvey-Jones, who called his book *Making it Happen*, also faced a difficult situation. ICI, one of the world's chemical giants, was going to suffer losses in the third quarter of 1980. It was only the second time in the company's history that such a thing had happened. ICI was very different from SAS—capital-intensive, with plants scattered all over the globe, a significant technology content and 20,000 employees. It is not easy to imagine the inertia of an economic unit of such size and structure.

However, Harvey-Jones' book is more a reflection on a managing process with heavy emphasis on change than a description of a series of concrete decisions that helped turn ICI around during his chairmanship. The styles that Harvey-Jones proposes for achieving business success, from the security—as he puts it—of having seen for himself that they work, have much in common with what can be perceived from Carlzon's actions. Harvey-Jones is a devout follower of the maxim that 'best is the enemy of good' (which reminds us of our recommendation to settle for suboptimizing in turnaround operations) and emphasizes action over excess analysis. For him, strategy should be a general outline of where one is headed towards than a complete, perfectionist vision. Strategy must be developed as one goes along, using an iterative analysis process that takes into account general trends (top downwards) and the company's reality at any one time (bottom upwards).

He maintains that it is important to keep the company on a change continuum. This, in turn, requires an open and frank style, prompt communication and sharing of responsibilities across layers of management, and demands a lot from people, setting ambitious but realistic goals, and a considerable degree of delegation and autonomy in the implementation. Harvey-Jones also stresses the importance of communication inside the company and the need to avoid barriers to this communication, which are often involuntarily raised when there are too many steps in the command pyramid.

Another point discussed by John Harvey-Jones is the management provided by the board of directors, which is a key element for maintaining a change culture in the company. Consensus by dialogue, constructive attitudes, participation and risk-sharing are fundamental. Mr Harvey-Jones' concern for the board of directors reminds us of the role that this institution can play both to maintain decline and to contest it. If the board is composed of yes-men, then without doubt we have an effective system for facilitating the mechanisms we have described in earlier chapters: decay and self-deception. In times of peace, it is particularly appropriate to reflect on the composition of the board of directors and one of the important aspects that should be nurtured in this composition is the inclusion of 'decline sensors'. These are people who will not feel comfortable in a deteriorating situation, people who tend not to accept self-deception, people who perhaps do not need to be members of that board and who are therefore prepared to risk their continued membership, if necessary, by saying what they think.

In the United States, it is becoming difficult to find good directors. In Europe, and especially in Spain, it is probably even more difficult. Sometimes, great efforts are made and a lot of money is spent on head hunters to find high-level managers, only to fill up the board of directors using superficial criteria. Few companies will escape from the odd difficult time when sharp direction changes are required and it is good for the senior management to have a source of warning, support and help in the board.

The specific steps taken by John Harvey-Jones in ICI during the early 1980s, which he does not describe in detail in his book, are recounted by Joseph Bower in his 1986 book *When Markets Quake*, which is an excellent study of the worldwide restructuring of the petrochemical industry. Bower, Harvard Business School professor and a known authority on the petrochemical industry, carried out a documented analysis of the restructuring of a series of petrochemical companies (Union Carbide, Dow

Chemical, British Petroleum, Imperial Chemical Industries, Shell and Montedison) and of the petrochemical industry in a series of countries (United States, France, Germany and Japan). From this analysis, Professor Bower generalizes his 'restructuring agenda for managers' as a series of practical recommendations. The first step, according to Bower, is to create in the company the ability to produce profits, which requires designing a strategy and reorganizing operations. The second step consists of simplifying the management structure at the top, reducing it to a small group of supermanagers with four main functions: mentors, sponsors, surgeons and architects. The third step, rationalization, is the turnaround process *per se*, as it has been approached in this book, and includes the resizing, combining, separating, closing, selling, refinancing, etc, operations we have described.

Joseph Bower suggests that, in many cases, turnarounds are only possible at industry level, that is as a cooperation process between companies competing in the industry, which is impossible if there is a very aggressive anti-trust policy. However, when industry-wide rationalizations are required, the chances are that the government will intervene, imposing political criteria which can produce a state of 'rationalizing from the irrational'. In the almost inevitable negotiations with the politicians that take place during a major restructuring, Bower says that managers should equip themselves with a supply of 'catalysing' experts.

Finally, Professor Bower stresses the leadership skills of the executive responsible for the turnaround. He must be able to carry along with him his managers and all the employees but must also be able to reach parties outside the company who may influence the process.

There are many other similar books that describe and analyse turnaround processes. Robert Shook, for example, in his 1990 book *Turnaround*, offers a detailed study of the revitalization of the Ford Motor Company during the 1980s. Ford lost 3.3 billion between 1980 and 1983. After the problems suffered by Chrysler, a fatalistic attitude predominated in Detroit: 'Now it's Ford's turn.' The leader in this case was Philip Caldwell who succeeded to Henry Ford as chairman in March 1980. The action was centred above all in Ford USA as Ford Europe was doing reasonably well during those years. Working in an enormous organization, impregnated from the early years of the century with a harsh culture in which people were little more than cogs in an industrial machine, what Caldwell did was basically to change this culture over a short period of time. The company had to question the Ford way of doing things and learn from the Japanese competitors who were taking the market out from under their feet.

Employees from all levels in Ford started to visit Nissan, Toyota, Honda and Mazda plants in Japan. A personal integration action was launched to get people to contribute their abilities, initiative and creativity to their jobs. Quality circles were started up. An entire integration and participation philosophy was put together, the MVGP (mission, values and guiding principles) programme. The integration was extended to include suppliers, stressing quality by means of a supplier rating system in the so-called Q1 (quality comes first) programme.

The company improved its negotiating style with the unions. In the early 1980s, Ford managers and leaders from the automobile union (AUW) together visited Japanese factories to get an idea on methods and potential for improving productivity and quality. This cooperation, which improved the understanding between the two sides, enabled a labour agreement lasting two and a half years to be achieved and which was a key factor in the company's revitalization effort.

Philip Caldwell was also a good communicator, as Robert Shook relates in his book, transmitting the ideas of his turnaround effort directly in the production plant, or indirectly through the press. But Caldwell also encouraged many other people in the Ford organization to communicate. Before the 1980s, any possibility of spending time on communication would have been considered as a cause of losing production and would have been avoided. In Caldwell's culture, communication became a vital part of teamwork, of personal integration and of the search for a creative contribution at all levels.

Another interesting book studying the revitalization of a number of large North American corporations is the 1987 book *The Leading Edge*, by Mark Potts and Peter Behr. The achievement of John Welch Jr at the head of General Electric, whose method was to focus the company on those fields in which it could be a leading competitor and pull out of those in which it could not excel, is one of the cases studied in depth. One of Welch's great decisions was the purchase of RCA, but this was only possible, among other things, thanks to RCA president Thornton Bradshaw's reorganization of the company, lopping off the excess branches acquired during diversification. This case too is studied by Potts and Behr, as is also that of Martin Marietta, whose president, Thomas Pownall, revitalized the company after the attempted takeover led by Bendix, using as his jumpoff point the company's main strengths: its technology and its skill in negotiating with government customers. In a turnaround process, it is important to identify the sick organization's strengths which can be used as an anchoring point for making the turnaround.

William Ylvisaker, the president of Gould, transformed a company with a rather mature position in the electrical equipment and automobile component industries by significantly increasing the technological content of its products. Howard Love adopted a different strategy to revitalize a giant such as National Steel, which was also trapped in a segment with a marked product maturity. Love spun off a plant, transferring the ownership to its employees, and grouped the other steel activities into a company whose ownership was shared with Nippon Kokan, one of Japan's leading steel companies. Love launched National Intergroup, the successor of the steel company, which operated in the crude oil transportation and pharmaceutical product distribution sectors. Love's approach would fit in the model we have called transplant turnaround.

GENERAL APPROACHES

Other authors suggest a series of concrete proposals to be applied in corporate turnaround projects. They are often authors with a wide experience as consultants, who reflect their experience by organizing such projects from an action-driven standpoint. Marvin Davis is one of these consultants who, in his 1987 book Turnaround, proposes a kind of guide for revitalizing companies. Table 8.1 provides a summary of the proposals that Davis discusses in his book. It is probably too summarized to do sufficient justice to the arsenal of recommendations offered in the book but it gives the reader an idea of the approach used.

Michael Beer, Rusell Eisenstat and Bert Spector (the first two are Harvard Business School professors) recommend a 'soft'* model in their 'critical turnaround path' in their 1990 book *The Critical Path to Corporate Renewal*. Table 8.2 shows the concept devised by Beer and his co-authors. This model, which seems to have sprung from the scientific field of organizational development, is based on the study of six turnarounds of large companies. The concept's emphasis is on revitalizing the people in the organization, improving their motivation and helping them to move themselves and things towards a vision of the target company (turned around) that is shared by everyone. The process consists of a balanced combination of careful pressure from above and acceptance of stimuli from below, generating a change in the right direction. The critical path method is probably more useful for tuning up a company that has become a little sleepy than for turning around a company in a serious state of decay. An approach such as this needs time but, in any case, it is interesting to read the opinion of a group of researchers who warn repeatedly against revitalization programmes pushed vigorously and exclusively from the top downwards.

---

* Soft means that the emphasis is placed on the human factor area of the company with a view to stimulating and improving motivation.

Table 8.1 *Summary of recommendations for revitalizing a company*

---

1. Clarify your objectives.
2. Clarify your authority and your company's decision process. Make sure that everyone understands where you want to go.
3. Clarify your strengths and weaknesses.
4. Formulate your pricing policy with special care.
5. Control your cash and financial policy.
6. Use financial analysis to identify excessive costs and control key areas.
7. Use people integrally.
8. Decide how you want the market to perceive your company and design your marketing policy accordingly.
9. Motivate customers and suppliers to buy and sell more.
10. Analyse the value contributed by your products and make sure that the right cost is attained.
11. Operate your factory like a business.
12. Communicate, communicate, communicate.
13. Develop an R&D plan that matches your strategy.
14. Take into account overseas markets.
15. Adapt these general principles to the circumstances of your company.
16. Bring it all together in a three-year plan.

Table 8.2 *Key steps along the critical path*

---

1. Mobilize energy for change among all the relevant parties in the organization by involving them in the diagnosis of the problems that impede competitiveness.
2. Develop a vision that is adapted to people's functions of how to organize oneself and aim for competitiveness.
3. Encourage the consensus that the new vision is correct, the competence to implement it and the cohesion to facilitate the change.
4. Extend the revitalization to all the unit's departments in order to avoid the perception that a programme is being pushed down from above, while also ensuring consistency with the organizational changes that are already in progress.
5. Consolidate the changes with formal policies, systems and structures that institutionalize the revitalization.
6. Continuously monitor and formulate a strategy in response to predictable problems from the revitalization process.

Another Harvard Business School professor, this time Quinn Mills, approaches the problem from the perspective of debureaucratizing the company in his 1991 book *Rebirth of the Corporation*. Professor Quinn Mills says that the hierarchical structures, the excessive bureaucratic formalism and the rigid policies that govern most companies' operations prevent their employees and managers from effectively applying their talents to solving problems and steering their company creatively adapted to the pressures of its environment.

Quinn Mills proposes his cluster organization concept,* in which people are grouped oriented towards a goal: 'clusters succeed because they enable the company to recruit better people, develop an ongoing commitment to quality, respond quickly to market changes and provide a fast-acting revitalization process when performance falls off'. Quinn Mills' clusters are not like many authors' task forces, in which a number of people with absolutely hierarchized and bureaucratic responsibilities are assigned temporarily and normally part-time to a group that will try to solve a specific problem. Quinn Mills' clusters, which replace the hierarchical organization, are a new form of organization. Table 8.3 shows Quinn Mills' seven steps for creating a cluster organization.

Table 8.3 *The seven steps for creating a cluster organization*

- Start at the top
- Undertake dramatic initial actions
- Speak with the troops in the front line
- Refine the 'vision'
- Review the organization's practices in the light of the 'vision'
- Define the clusters and work on the organization's limitations
- Communicate with the middle managers

The first step is obviously the support of the chief executive of the business unit (company or division). Dramatic actions are aimed at sending a clear message to the entire organization that things are going to change (like in the 'moment of truth'), for

---

* The term 'cluster' is used more when things are grouped by extrinsic causes than when they themselves decide to group together, in which case they would be a 'group' or 'association'. Michael Porter also has a concept using this word 'clusters of excellence' which refers to when several companies achieve excellence by competing between each other, as may be the case with Mercedes Benz and BMW or Toyota and Nissan. In early 1991, an attempt was made to apply the concept of clusters or excellence in the Basque Country. Some employers understood that perhaps the government would give money to those who were in the cluster and there was a sudden increase in interest in Michael Porter in the Basque Country.

example a staff cut. The third step, speak with the organization's lower levels, seeks to integrate them in the process and establish a fluid vertical communication.

The next task is to centre the 'vision' of how the company should be after the reorganization and achieve a broad level of agreement on this 'vision' among key managers. The fifth step is to find the parallelism between strategy, structure and people's behaviour. Everything must be consistent, but this consistency can be looked for from any of these levels, that is first encouraging the right behaviour and then introducing the cluster structure or vice versa, as the process leader's criterion dictates, following a line of minimum resistance.

The sixth and perhaps most important step is precisely the organization of the clusters; the purpose is to put into motion a participative process to establish the clusters, in accordance with the employees, around missions, important activities and specific production or service tasks. Finally, the seventh step requires that the senior management involved in transforming a bureaucratic organization into a cluster organization maintain close communication with their middle managers, technicians and staff. In fact, one of the advantages of the cluster organization is the greater communication between its members—a network of communication, in all directions, instead of the limited vertical communication of the conventional organization.

Quinn Mills' concepts are innovative and the professor provides a number of success stories in revitalizing business units in different international contexts. However, it also seems to us that this approach could be more valuable in keeping the company healthy, alert and on its guard than in solving a difficult situation. In the turnaround, as in medicine, there are different levels of therapy for different levels of severity. We know that it is possible to treat preventively something as serious as a heart attack (no smoking, watch cholesterol, do exercise) but once the heart attack has happened, this treatment is no longer useful.

In an interesting article published in 1990 in the *Journal of Business Strategy*, Geoffrey Lurie and Joseph Ahearn offer a nine-point recipe for companies in difficulties that is more in line with the certain feeling of urgency we have operated within in this book. The reader will remember the famous cabbage patch dolls of the 1980s. This highly successful rag doll was launched by a company called Coleco. This company rapidly achieved $400 million in sales but set out on a series of takeovers and diversifications that landed it with very high overheads. Coleco went bankrupt, tried to restructure itself, and finally disappeared. The authors study this unfortunate failure in some depth and propose the list of recommendations given in Table 8.4.

Table 8.4 *Lurie and Ahearn's nine points for turning around a company*

---

1. Identify the basic cause of the problem.
2. Apply a strong and effective leadership.
3. Treat the difficult problems quickly.
4. Do not look for solutions outside the areas of competence of the people comprising the turnaround team.
5. Keep pressure applied on the process.
6. Remember that the threat of a difficult action is worse than the action itself.
7. Turn negative aspects into positive aspects.
8. Always have an alternative plan ready.
9. Remember that when one has nothing to lose, one has everything to win.

These authors clearly follow a 'hard'* approach; they provide recommendations that stress actions aimed at attacking problems urgently, without any long periods of doubting reflection, suboptimizing and only doing what one already knows how to do.

---

* Rather than acting indirectly on people's motivation so that they 'change gear', the idea is to act directly on the problems to solve them.

Frederick Zimmerman, director of management advanced training programmes in the University of St Thomas, in St Paul, Minnesota, but with a considerable wealth of experience in industry and specifically in turnaround cases, published in 1991 an interesting book based on the in-depth analysis of 16 corporate turnaround situations, some of which were successful and some were not. Zimmerman groups the turnaround attempts into three categories:

1. those that use a tactic of reducing operating costs;
2. those that use a tactic of product differentiation; and
3. those that use tactics that stress leadership (improve motivation).

Zimmerman's book is well argued and some of his conclusions are very interesting. Thus, for example, he finds that the company's size does not seem to be an important factor for the problem concerning us. He also points out that the companies which turned around successfully were more effective in the operations area than those that failed. The example of the management team accepting salary cuts in order to facilitate cost improvement is another aspect that is related with successful turnarounds. The companies that managed to turn around through product differentiation often emphasized their products' quality as a distinctive factor. One salient point in the companies that approached turnaround from the leadership perspective was the continuity of the team responsible for the process and their experience in the ailing company's industry.

To summarize, Table 8.5 shows the variables identified by Zimmerman for each of his three categories. As in life, there are no chemically pure situations in the company and a certain combination of elements of all three categories is possible.

Although he did not write his 1987 book with the turnaround primarily in mind, John Gabarro, another Harvard Business School professor, admits that he has received many comments from people related in one way or another with this problem on the considerable applicability of the ideas he develops in the book. Gabarro finds that when a manager takes up new responsibilities he needs a certain amount of time before he sufficiently understands the business to take decisions that are able to influence specific aspects of the ways of competing in a certain industry. This may seem a truism but Gabarro explores this finding in greater depth with a view to precisely quantifying and qualifying it.

Table 8.5 *Turnaround categories and main variables of each category*

Cost reduction tactic
- Operational efficiency
- Effective stock management
- Reduction of overheads
- Design for cost reduction.

Product differentiation tactic
- Differentiating features
- Reliability and performance
- Product quality
- Continuity on market.

Leadership enhancing tactic
- Focus on operations
- Stability of management team
- Experience in industry
- Technical experience
- Internal consistency and with the company's resources
- Incremental changes
- Ethical attitude.

A good generalist manager is able to appreciate problem areas that will benefit from certain changes when he takes on these new responsibilities. This, we could add, would surely be more so in turnaround cases when the business unit is affected by collective self-deception. Therefore, it is easy for people who take on new responsibilities to immediately take some major decisions. However, a certain period of time must pass for those generalist managers *also* to become specialist managers in the specific business of the business unit of which they are in charge. Once this specialization has been achieved, they will dare to undertake another series of important changes, but this time more closely matched to the business.

Gabarro finds a certain model of behaviour in decision-taking involving major organizational changes in the unit the manager has joined. This model has three peaks which Gabarro, based on the data of his study, quantifies as follows:

- the first peak occurs three months after taking up the new post and averages somewhat more than four organizational changes;
- the second peak occurs eighteen months after taking up the new job (average time required to acquire the specialization to manage the unit in that business) and averages about five changes;
- the third peak appears after thirty months and averages two changes.

This finding is consistent with Zimmerman's suggestion about the stability of the management team and with Laurie and Ahearn's remark about avoiding looking for solutions that require skills that are not held by the members of the turnaround team.

The recession that followed the second oil shock, when neither the general economy nor most of the business world had yet assimilated the first shock, led many companies to undertake turnaround projects during the early 1980s. Therefore, those years were a good laboratory for observing managers at work on such a difficult task. Some employers approached the turnaround process from a peculiar philosophical perspective. They wished to transplant a small company culture into the large company, inject into the large corporation doses of entrepreneurship business initiative at all levels, in order thus to achieve a rapid process of change. Perhaps the most influential work in this category was the book written by Howard Pinchot in 1985, whose title *Intrapreneurship* became a key word during those years. If an entrepreneur is able to found and make his company grow, often without economic resources, almost always alone, and without a record or an assets base or much else on which to support himself, then how much easier must it be for a company manager to ensure the success of his division, product, branch or whatever other unit he is responsible for. Indeed, managers have all the protection that belonging to a company confers on them, as well as having access to the company's internal resources. One of the many examples that Pinchot discusses in his book is that of the famous 'Post-it', the yellow stickers marketed by 3M that we all use with the typical 'in case it should interest you' when we want to curry our boss's favour by sending him an article that might give him an idea for his next speech. If Mr Art Fry, who was the 'intrapreneur' who could be considered as leading the launch of this product, had had to form his own company to do so, it is possible that it would have taken him many years, and it is possible that he would have failed. By developing the product inside 3M, he had access to the best adhesives technology in the world, an internationally renowned brandname, funds to finance rapid development and a blanket launch, and international distribution channels.

Obviously, if it is possible to stimulate all the potential entrepreneurs in a company to 'intrapreneur' and the cultural and corporate systems are created to allow and sustain the phenomenon, then a revitalizing revolution is created and this can be used to turn around companies. It is a very suggestive idea and many management committees are prepared to pay a lot of money to hear it from the lips of Pinchot or other intrapreneurship gurus. My opinion is that a certain dose of it is a tonic to keep a company healthy and to wake up any company that has fallen asleep, but it would seem very rash to me to propose to turn around a company using these methods.

The books published by Rosabeth Moss Kanter (1983 and 1989), now in the Harvard Business School, or those of her colleagues in the same school John Kotter (1990) and Quinn Mills (1985), are on the same lines. All of them concentrate on suggesting practical ideas for speeding up the management of declining companies. Whether this be by encouraging entrepreneurship, or with suitable leadership styles, or with informal grids, or with a wide range of variations on these approaches, these authors pour into their books an enormous wealth of experience and relevant experiences to get more out of organizations. By way of oversimplified summary, their message stresses the need to facilitate the full development of people, to get them to deploy all their skills by encouraging environments in which learning is ongoing and in which risk is accepted over bureaucracy.

The literature on change is not new but these authors offer the most contemporary views on how to approach the problem. As in other cases, I think that their ideas, although generally proposed as a remedy in turnaround cases, are good prescriptions for keeping the healthy company in good shape and preventing it from falling ill, but are unlikely to generate drastic changes in the general trend in a short period of time.

REVITALIZING COMPANIES IN JAPAN

A ny searching review of modern literature must inevitably include an analysis of the problem in Japanese companies. Corporate decline is a virus that also attacks Japanese companies and may even kill them. However, the business environment in Japan has certain antibodies that considerably hinder the micro-organism's corrosive work.

The protective umbrella of the state, through the MITI, is one of these factors. The long-term view of Japanese employers, which leads them to sacrifice profits today if necessary for better profits tomorrow, is another. The interface between companies and banking and the latter's ability to understand the former is the third factor. The industrial structuring in clusters, in which larger companies accept a certain degree of responsibility for other smaller companies, in exchange for the latter accepting to contribute flexibility to the former, is another differentiating factor that influences decline and turnaround in Japan. Finally, the Japanese companies' particular skill in competing and cooperating is another differentiating factor. Indeed, if a Japanese company discovers that a certain activity performed by another company may be relevant for implementing its strategy, it is very likely that it will attempt to establish some type of business relationship with that company rather than try to force it out of the market or purchase it and integrate it into its system.

Professor Carl Kester of the Harvard Business School analysed in 1991 a few cases of reorganization in Japan, discussing in some detail that of his flagship company Nippon Steel. Kester shows that even the Japanese fall asleep (in the entrepreneurial sense, as we all know that they are better trained than most Westerners to do so physiologically). Even on the top of the great tower of one the largest companies in the world, under the scrutinizing gaze of all, Nippon Steel fell asleep, accumulated too many workers, watched its stocks and its accounts receivable grow and also, as is logical, its indebtedness. It was not able to foresee the decline of construction and shipbuilding in Japan nor the decreased use of steel in cars, nor the pressure of the higher quality steels made by other manufacturers. As a result, even Nippon Steel had to admit in the early 1980s that the moment of truth had come.

In Japanese corporate turnaround plans, however, there is one factor stressed by Kester and other authors that is enormously differentiating: the effort to keep jobs. Kester asserts that the Japanese employer's contract with his workers seems to be stronger than with his shareholders. In order to save jobs, Japanese companies resort to two main strategies, diversification and expansion abroad, first via exports and then by any other approach (technical assistance, direct investment abroad). These two strategies take time and it is the shareholders and the banks that bear the brunt of the sacrifices.

The 'big group' approach or cluster of companies also serves this purpose. If a company has 1,000 too many workers, then the problem is to distribute them among all the companies in a group. A thousand workers too many will cause any operating account to founder and sharing them out may need more imagination than Cervantes; however, if they are distributed in small doses among subcontractors, suppliers, customers and other companies in a big group, it is possible to digest them.

In his recommendations in 1988 for revitalizing Japanese construction companies, Fumio Hasegawa suggests six approaches: international deployment, diversification (which, as we have already said, are typical turnaround remedies used by the Japanese company), integration of construction and engineering, technological development and the use of financial engineering to be able to undertake assignments by mobilizing funds on the capital market. In this case too the problem is spread over a long time horizon during which the company will not fall because it will be held up between its creditors and shareholders or because, if things should come to the very worst, the government will do something since it is pro-industrial (the Japanese do not know how lucky they are) and that is what it is there for.

If we go to the medium-sized but independent company, we find a situation very similar to that in Europe or the United States. In his 1989 account of the history of the machine-tool leader MAZAK, Yasumori Kuba explains that to cope with a production–demand mismatch, the company organized a 'sales caravan', turning engineers, middle managers, technicians and other indirect employees into salesmen and providing them with a small vehicle loaded with a machine from the inventory so that they could demonstrate it and, preferably, sell it. The second step taken by MAZAK was to export aggressively. The flight forwards tends to be the Japanese's favourite method to restore their companies' health and, more often than not, their flight path usually leads them to Europe and the United States.

Approaches based on leadership and business initiative also have their place in Japan. Kuniyasu Sakai is a philosopher of the corporate breakdown. Like a Japanese Schumacher, Sakai defines himself as a 'Great Master of the Sakai Management School', which consists of applying his *Bunsha* philosophy of corporate breakdown (Sakai and Sekiyama, 1989). Sakai formed the company which would later become Taiyo Kogyo, a holding company consisting of 34 companies in different industries (three of them in the printed circuits sector supplied, in 1985, 11 per cent of the Japanese market).

The *Bunsha* philosophy implies spinning off units from the company as independent enterprises. By splitting up the company, one gives life to men, Mr Sakai never tires of telling us. Companies which give life to others share in its capital. The

157

new business cells may cooperate or compete with their mother cells. As Sakai says, 'The important thing is the DNA, the genetic code that remains alive.' The art of *Bunsha* is knowing when to cut and to whom to assign responsibility. Sakai has created a foundation to spread his *Bunsha* philosophy about revitalization by division. He has published a book which has been translated into many languages and which he distributes free to explain his philosophy. He himself has retired from the foundation's management, which is in the hands of professionals, but remains as director, philosopher and master and spends part of his life and enormous energy in spreading his ideas all over the world.

Another Japanese author, Keitaro Hasegawa, gives an additional perspective on the attitude of senior Japanese managers in declining companies (Hasegawa, 1986). Indeed, the fact that the company or even the entire sector to which the company belongs is in decline does not discourage managers from continuing to invest in R&D. The R&D investment made by Japanese companies in primary industrial sectors such as steel, textiles, non-ferrous metals, ceramics, wood and paper, in the early 1980s, accounted for somewhat more than 12 per cent of the entire industry's total expenditure in research and development. On the other hand, the same industrial sectors in the United States only invested about 4 per cent of the entire industry's total investment in R&D.

The government must share part of the blame in this (in both parts of the world), in Japan because of the role played by the MITI as the true artist and conductor of a comprehensive industrial policy,* in the United States because the state, either as buyer or subsidiser, has chosen to abandon certain sectors in

---

* The eternal debate in the West on whether 'industrial policy yes or industrial policy no' would benefit extraordinarily from studying the role of the Japanese MITI. I do not think that anyone can doubt the correctness of this industrial policy based on forecasting, planning, influence, agreement, and direct and indirect support. Daniel Okimoto, a University of Stanford professor, has recently published an excellent book on the role of the MITI (Okimoto, 1989). For a discussion of the consensus policy and a very interesting and up-to-date analysis of the Japanese economic phenomenon, see Isamu Miyazaki (1990).

favour of others—although it finances more than one-third of the R&D expenditure of so-called advanced sectors, it does not even cover 5 per cent of the total R&D expenditure by the sectors we call declining. In Europe, the situation is closer to that of the United States than to Japan.

The result of this is that the economy's mature sectors are much less mature in Japan than in the United States or Europe. Hence the reason why the Japanese steel industry is consolidating positions throughout the world, the Japanese textile industry is starting to spread abroad and the other mature sectors will probably do the same.

In his book on Honda, Robert Shook (1988) also explains how declining Western companies immediately cut down on R&D expenditure when they consider that the 'moment of truth' has come, while Japanese companies also reduce expenditure in all areas but try to maintain their R&D spending. To what extent is this the result of a business outlook genetically committed to the long term? To what extent is it the result of a possible certainty that the company will not disappear because that is not in the country's plans? We can only look at the facts and the results.

CONCLUSION

I n recent years, there has been an abundant accumulation of ideas, concepts and techniques related to the problem of corporate turnaround. Turning around a company—as will be readily understood—means different things to different authors. The main variable determining the differences in what each author finds and/or recommends seems to be the urgency of the turnaround and, consequently, the degree of deterioration suffered by the business unit concerned. Surprisingly enough, most authors never mention this variable (how far gone the company to be turned around is). On many occasions, when they include portions of their databases in their books, either because they base their presentation on particular cases or because the situations are widely known, it is possible to infer what kind of turnaround the author has in mind.

Table 8.6 gives a classification—by no means comprehensive—of differential features deduced from our review of the literature, based on the degree of urgency of the turnaround. Seen from this viewpoint, one would expect the two columns to complement each other. It could be said that the right-hand column is the preventive remedy and the left-hand column is the curative remedy. If one fails, we will have to resort to the other but if, after curing, we forget to continue the preventive therapy, we will have to go back to the first column. With this proviso, the important contribution selected from the literature is reconciled with the proposals of this book, whose focus, as the reader knows, has been above all on turning around companies whose health is already severely impaired.

Table 8.6 *Some differential features of turnarounds depending on the urgency*

Urgent turnaround: very serious situation	Turnaround advisable: situation of moderate decline
• The turnaround team diagnoses and acts	• The turnaround team encourages participative diagnosis, distributed decision and responsibility-taking
• Drastic action	• Incremental and progressive action
• General action (adjustment to the situation, not to the business)	• Specific action (adjustment to the business)
• Act on: product, price, cost, balance sheet, system structure and/or design (hard)	• Act on: culture and/or motivation (soft)
• Objectives primarily quantifiable in money and time (short term)	• Objectives primarily qualitative (medium/long term)
• Emphasis on controlling fund flow	• Emphasis on organizational development

9

Conclusion

I n this last chapter, I will try to synthesize some of the most important ideas and concepts that have appeared in this book, both those harvested from my own research and experience and those others which I consider backed by a solid body of evidence and reflection. I am well aware that writing a chapter of conclusions is an invitation to the reader pressed for time to skip the other chapters, and who knows if he will even finish this one. In this book, I have sought both to support the ideas and concepts and to express them widely and fully by surrounding them with real-life experiences in which these ideas and concepts manifest themselves with all their ramifications and relationships, as is the natural way of things in reality. Obviously, in this chapter, the ideas and concepts will be presented much more simply.

CHANGE SENSORS

T hink of the last car you have ridden in. Perhaps it was a sophisticated Mercedes Benz of the latest series or a simple Mini of the type they are now starting to build again. Both of them are packed with sensors that constantly monitor the cooling water temperature, the oil pressure, the battery charge, the fuel level, speed, and, if we are talking about the more sophisticated vehicle, dozens of parameters more. In fact, many of the improvements in vehicle performance have come about because more variables are being monitored and automatic ways have been found to respond immediately to deviations from the norm.

In a company, it is also possible to monitor hundreds of parameters, although a few well-chosen ones will always guarantee control. Ongoing monitoring of parameters such as cash flow, return, market share, debt–equity ratio, etc., may immediately reveal a process of deterioration. We have seen many other signs of decline in the course of this book.

In order to monitor the key parameters we have chosen, we need sensors. The best way to calibrate parameters of corporate health is to contrast them with the most efficient competitor. It is vital to know what value these parameters must have when the company is healthy. The ideal situation is that in which the sensors are like the modern sensors based on smart chips, which take their own corrective decisions on the basis of the information they sense (no doubt that is why they are called smart, because they correct). This would be the case if we had succeeded in implementing a culture of automatic responsibility-taking, to the point that anybody in the organization would react automatically to the least deviation in performance. Unfortunately, this is to be found in very few organizations but it is always possible to define and communicate the objectives and what is really happening so that everyone knows how the company, and how that part of the company for which a particular person is responsible, is doing.

DECISION

When one looks at a company that has been slowly sliding downhill year after year, one comes to imagine that its managers must think like a driver who sees little red lights on his car's dashboard on the part indicating the state of the brakes, among other things, who sees the speedometer indicating 100 miles per hour, and says that the instruments must be out of order.

As soon as things show the least symptom of decline, the word is: action. Action should be suboptimizing. Professor

Lorenzo Dionis, of the IESE, is reminded by his colleagues of a military phrase he used to use when referring to this type of action in teachers' meetings: 'See a machine-gun, shoot it up.' Indeed, in a military advance, if one discovers an enemy machine-gun, it is not the time to start analysing whether it is manned or not, or whether they would be willing to surrender, or whether they are asleep. It can do a lot of damage and one must not lose even a second.

It must be very difficult to implement a turnaround plan because many managers are unable to do so even when the press is crying out for it. If it was an easy decision, a lot less would have been written on the subject. But the reader will agree that it is a sad thing to be famous for not having taken the decision. There are boards that have to change company president two or three times until they find one who is prepared to acknowledge that the 'moment of truth' has come. When the president is the owner and the company is starting to plummet, then we have a problem without any solution.

The ability to take the decision to turn around the company, in spite of it being what it is, is fundamental and therefore we have seen that the prolonged, collective self-deception can and must be avoided and that mechanisms should be prepared to facilitate taking this type of decision when necessary. One of these mechanisms is the creation of a suitable board of directors.

VISION OF THE RESTRUCTURED COMPANY

A turnaround manager must know where he is going. He must be able to formulate a vision of how the company or business unit to be restructured will be at a certain time in the future, which I could perhaps set at three years from now. The person leading this type of project must be able to define the design the company will then have: what size and its configuration (one big plant or several small plants), what degree of vertical integration, what degree of flexibility, what location, what technology. He must define what products it will have, what markets it will compete in and with what strategy: price, differentiation, service, quality, range, performance, etc.

He must be able to define what balance sheet and what income statement his business unit will then have. The more precise this vision can be, the better, because he will have to explain it and move towards it.

A turnaround is not like claypigeon-shooting. It is not a matter of knocking down one problem after another, wherever they may come from. It is a process of solutions leading in a particular direction.

HUMAN TEAM

Only you, dear reader, have superpowers. All the other managers that people the world's economy are normal people who sometimes make mistakes, sometimes become obfuscated, know more about some things than other things and about some things they know nothing at all, who want to go on vacation from time to time, can fall ill and may even send it all to hell and look for fresh pastures.

So, if the turnaround problem affects you, perhaps we need not worry. But I can assure you that if it affects any other businessman or woman, then I can only hope he is able to find a suitable team of normal people.

Turnarounds are not one-man jobs. And as normal people have so many limitations, organizing a team is not easy, but it is extremely important. For anyone who is not the reader, acquiring superpowers is impossible. However, organizing a super-team, a team that does have superpowers, is more feasible, as each member will contribute what others lack.

The more powerful the team is, the more difficult it is to manage it. In fact, any team is only powerful if it is managed. A turnaround leader should be in balance with the human team he chooses. When organizing and motivating this team, it is important to keep in mind what can happen further on, when the company is more healthy or even unrecognizably restructured, because it would be a pity if success were to burn out the team.

MODELS AND EXPERIENCE

In the 1990s and beyond, we have accumulated a considerable body of experience in reorganizing, restructuring, turning around or whatever we want to call the phenomenon we are studying. This experience, recorded in an abundant literature, can be classified on the basis of various criteria. We have considered two major categories: turnaround by breaking down and transplanting, and turnaround by generalized revitalization. We have also introduced the most commonly used models for implementing these types of process.

We academics like to create categories, groups, models (and then put them on colour transparencies so that the audience can say 'Oooh!'). I do not know if this is what we should be doing. Cutting reality up into slices may be a way of understanding it better. But reality does not come in slices but *en masse*. That is why those who are able to analyse and decide in three dimensions have an advantage over those who can only do it in two or one dimension. When the academics recommend that a model be followed—that which the manager's ability to carry out an analysis/synthesis establishes as the most suitable—it is because it helps to be more consistent, it helps the entire human team to understand better how some things fit in with others, so that the process can be seen as something consistent too. The people we have called stakeholders need to perceive this consistency. But as reality has many dimensions, we should also be prepared to combine models.

In order to advance towards the vision that has been built up of the restructured company, a concrete plan containing quantified actions must be drawn up: a kind of turnaround PERT. It is at this point that it is useful to have some principle that will provide the backbone for the entire process: we are going to reduce the cost, differentiate the product, make the company flexible, expand the market abroad, etc. If there are priority objectives, we could adopt a focused style; if we try to improve everything at once, in all directions, then we may perhaps create a certain amount of confusion.

The turnaround programme, which we have tentatively recommended should have a maximum duration of three years, should be well linked to a cash flow plan and this should be the main control instrument to which all the variables are referred.

NEGOTIATION AND AGREEMENT

I n order to make progress in implementing the PERT that models the turnaround process, many difficult decisions must be taken and put into action. In reality, these decisions can only be taken after lengthy negotiations and agreement as to their content. If the decision is to institute temporary layoffs, this decision cannot be implemented without having reached an agreement beforehand with the workers, with the workers' committee and, sometimes, with the unions (these three groups should be in agreement but it is not always so); of course, the employment authorities must also agree. When all these parties are in agreement, then the decision can be taken.

To shorten times, change shifts, modify task design, automate, decrease the workforce, close facilities, relocate geographically, redefine categories, restructure liabilities, improve collection conditions, transfer stock to suppliers, turn indirect labour into direct labour and for the entire arsenal of tools used to turn around companies, one must first negotiate, reach an agreement and then act with calmness and diligence.

The autocratic leader is unlikely to succeed in a turnaround. If he has an extraordinary charisma then perhaps he may but only at the risk of burning himself out in confrontation. The humble, tenacious, step-by-step approach that looks at all the possibilities is more recommendable. Corporate turnarounds have a lot in common with political processes and therefore skills in negotiating and obtaining agreements are crucial.

COMMUNICATION

I f at this point I should write, 'in turnarounds, communicate, communicate and communicate', I would not be saying anything and yet this is exactly what several authors have written. When the 'moment of truth' has passed and everyone knows that it is no longer possible to continue deceiving oneself, fear and uncertainty appear. Everyone wonders where the scalpel will cut. People's concern is not just limited to losing their job, but to a change of job, reporting to another job, ending up in a cul-de-sac. The concern, fed by rumours and false reports—when not by ill-intentioned messages—may give rise to inertias that work against the turnaround effort. That is why it is important to inform. 'Uncertainty hurts more than knowledge of the truth,' said one manager referring to that period of information vacuum in the transition from the decline to starting the turnaround process.

One clear recommendation: be one step ahead by informing. Nothing is more annoying than retaining information about what will be done and then reading it the next day twisted out of shape in the press. Nowadays, it is almost impossible to control information. One of a good manager's tasks is to practise the virtue of discretion and it is therefore wise to screen assistants so that one does not include those who become depressed if a week goes by without their photo appearing in the papers. But one must be realistic and not try to conceal what it is better that everyone knows. Proper communication is a powerful tool in a turnaround process.

MONITORING THE PROCESS: CASH FLOW CONTROL

S ome corporate revitalization processes consist of a feasibility plan and lots of money. These are above all the plans for state-run companies. One year later, the public realize that the feasibility plan was only the excuse to cover up the losses for a couple of years. This is increasingly less common in Europe and it is likely that it will disappear as the Single Market becomes consolidated. Most turnaround projects, however, do not have the privilege of the safety net of the state budget. It is more likely that during its decline the company will have consumed a large part of its resources and committed those it does not have with significant borrowing.

The cash flow plan is the best tool for monitoring the turnaround process. We have repeated this several times because it is extremely important. The impact of any action should be reflected in the plan. When we speak of cash flow in a turnaround process, we already know that we can understand it in a wide sense to be the funds available for the project, including the funds obtained from disposals and those which can be procured on the market for use in the process. The timetable should be kept to even though the difficulty of the decisions generates a multitude of arguments for postponing them.

The leaders of a turnaround process hold innumerable and exhausting meetings with their managers to 'push' the process through. They must be convinced, supported, helped to find the best way and to achieve the necessary consensus for grappling with complicated, high-risk dilemmas.

The team's cohesion, its commitment to the process, its stability, its professionalism, the successes achieved in the early stages, all have a positive effect on the availability of funds for the project. Management teams who are motivated and enthusiastic about a well-planned turnaround process have been able to raise large sums of money to finance it.

ETHICAL ISSUES

In the 1990s, one cannot publish anything without mentioning ethics. Even the instruction manuals of household appliances, which already talk about responsible use, will probably soon include a reference to the ethical relationship between the device and its user. Corporate turnaround is a subject that enables many references to be made to ethics. Revitalizing a company, avoiding the destruction of wealth and loss of jobs, is an intrinsically good task, but it is also highly complex and it is wise to filter the decisions that must be taken through criteria that ensure their morality.

One of the areas in which ethical problems are raised with greatest frequency is in the acceptance of responsibility. In declining companies, there sometimes comes a point when no one wants to be on the bridge when the ship goes under. The sale of stocks to heroic frontmen or to intermediary companies that carry out the same function is a common occurrence. If things work out, there are agreements that ensure that the ownership is returned to its original holders; if things do not work out, there are agreements that ensure that those who manage the bankruptcy receive suitable compensation. Approaching a turnaround process with excessive precautions to avoid possible liabilities if the process fails is hardly going to motivate the management team that has to cooperate in the project. No manager likes to be shut in a factory by his workers or have a sign stuck on his front door at home. Some accept the risk of that happening because they are convinced that they are fighting a righteous fight. But no good professional likes to be on the receiving end of such treatment when it should be going to someone else. The wounds that these things cause spoil relationships and people.

Another ethical problem area which is often involved in turnaround processes is the fair sharing out of the cost of the process and its possible benefits. In order to obtain the funds necessary to progress, payments must be postponed, debt renegotiated with suppliers (in certain cases reduction of this debt can be obtained in return for other compensations), new financing obtained from partners, the public (by increases in capital stock, for example, in the case of listed companies), or lenders. In such cases, one can either use 100 per cent of the truth, or a lower percentage of it. A management team may say that it is fully convinced that it will be able to successfully implement its turnaround plan but to what extent is it fair to take others along with it who cannot suitably assess the risk?

The information received by stockholders or holders of other investment instruments in listed companies is very little in most industrialized countries. No matter how much the authorities try to improve statutory reporting and limit transactions with inside information, the scandals that have broken out in the United States and Europe in the late 1980s and in Japan in the early 1990s are a sign of the considerable room for manoeuvre offered to agents and intermediaries by the lack of information on the identity of investors. Many turnaround programmes have benefited from funds provided by investors who were unaware of the risk associated with their funds and, obviously, were not suitably remunerated. If the reader should one day find himself in a board meeting in which disrespectful jokes are cracked about stockholders, he can rest assured that this is not the first time that this has happened. Perhaps we should advise him to resign from the board immediately?

We have said that turnaround processes are a succession of negotiations and agreements. On more than one occasion, the temptation appears of buying favours that cannot be won by arguments. Politicians, unionists, executives, agents can all be bought. There are those who are aware of their strength and are waiting to be bought. There are those who accept bribes due to weakness. Does the end of turning around a company justify bribing the workers' committee so that it can help smooth the path for a staff cut? There are employers who have no doubt in their mind that it is justified and admire the art of those who have attained such persuasive skills.

The most unpleasant phenomenon one can come across in the world of failing companies is the false saviour, the manager who has nothing to lose, who uses the company's crisis to his own benefit. Sometimes, these people gain the support of the company's employees—they are often past masters in getting it—who see in them their own lifeline. However, these people often use the workers as an argument with which to blackmail shareholders, creditors, major suppliers or the government, with the only goal of remaining at the head of the company and obtaining significant personal gains from it. A steel employer who had purchased a deeply troubled company saw some trucks transporting scrap that were about to leave. He asked someone to check what type of scrap it was. It was highly valuable machinery. The scrap merchant, in this case, was the manager responsible for the company until the day before.

I would be irresponsible if I were to try and cram in the recipe-book for ethical turnarounds in these paragraphs. However, there are a couple of recommendations I can give. The choice of the management team that will work on the project must be guided above all by the ethical criterion. Good professionals also tend to be honest. After all, professional executives depend basically on their reputation. A team of good professionals is not likely to start treading on slippery ground. Treating the typical dilemmas of turnaround processes in an open manner, involving the key executives in the discussion and decision-taking, helps find professional solutions and avoids immoral short-cuts.

The other recommendation is very simple: abide by the law. Although it is a very simple recommendation, it is not always easy to follow it. To help, the best solution is to have a good team of legal advisers. There are upright lawyers who dedicate their imagination and experience to helping the employer do things properly and there are shoddy lawyers who boast of being able to push anything through, no matter how shady it may be. It is not very difficult to tell the two apart and, often, simply the lawyer he has chosen is a good sign of whether the employer is working with good intentions or merely wants to get his own way.

PREVENTION

The final aspect of a turnaround should be avoiding having to use it again. There is a selfish reason for managers who have succeeded in engineering a turnaround for making sure that they do not have to do it again: there are very few cases in corporate history of managers who have managed to get their company out of two crises. There are many managers who have got several different companies out of a crisis, but not the same company. It is as if during the process of curing the company, the manager were to vaccinate it against him and when he tries to deploy his skill again, it simply does not work.

Prevention requires the ability to maintain change as a way of life in the company, of achieving ongoing learning and constant improvement with everyone's involvement. It also requires having alarm mechanisms at all levels (sensor monitoring, as we have recommended earlier on): from independent outside directors to responsible, well-trained and well-informed middle managers, able to vote with their feet if the situation deteriorates and a reorganization process is not provided immediately.

FINAL COMMENTS

It is said that one of the world's most renowned heart surgeons, Dr Cooley, from the famous Houston Medical Center, once performed an emergency operation on a patient who had received a gunshot wound in the chest in an accident. When he walked out of the operating theatre, with his usual calm and incredible self-assuredness, he told the shot man's wife, 'The operation has been a success but the patient has died.' Unlike employers, surgeons have the advantage of performing a large number of operations and, perhaps because of this, may gain considerable renown in spite of a few failures. The employers or executives who take on corporate turn-arounds cannot take Dr Cooley's stance. Indeed, just one failure may mean that they are never given an opportunity to try again and may even force them into early retirement.

As we have seen, any business activity affects growing numbers of stakeholders. The limiting counterweight effect that Marxist ideology has always had on business decisions, due to their acceptance by certain sectors in the corporate environment (unions, government, workers, communications media, etc) has disappeared to all practical purposes. However, social control on business activity is not only unlikely to disappear but may very possibly increase. This control will take on increasingly more complex forms (protection of the environment, provision of detailed and reliable information to the public, involvement in decision-taking, protection of minority owners, scrutiny of the use of inside information, etc).

The urgency and trauma of turnaround operations may bring them in head-on collision with the expectations of a large number of stakeholders. These conflicts may appear immediately or after a certain period of time has passed. It is possible that the conflicts carry with them legal liabilities and it is important to realize that the law will probably be applied with increasing strictness and that things that are tolerable today may not be so in a few years time. Indeed, it is possible that the increasing legal stringency may be applied retroactively in some cases. As a North American turnaround manager used to say, 'We are in a lawsuit-driven society, I don't even go to the bathroom without consulting with my lawyer first.' Without going to extremes, when commencing a turnaround it is a good idea to have a good adviser in company law, not to have him take decisions but so that he can help you take them in a legally correct manner.

Speaking of turnarounds, one can make a slightly cynical remark. The economic cycle is a reality and manifests itself in a specific manner in each industrial sector. We do not exactly know why but the fact is that since Biblical times there have been times of plenty and times of want. It is much easier to be a corporate genius, a super-turnarounder, when the economy is on the upslope than when it is crashing through the floor. The generalized euphoria during periods of prosperity encourages everyone to support the turnaround. In times of economic blues, one thinks more of the mistakes made when the money was pouring in, it becomes fashionable to be conservative and people doubt the ability to work corporate miracles. Therefore, if the reader is about to embark on revitalizing a company, he would be wise in considering beforehand the attitude he may find around him as a result of the prevailing economic situation.

Finally, I would like to insist on the considerable negotiating skills that must be deployed by those who undertake a major rationalization, reorganization or restructuring process. One must know how to identify the fronts of the problem that are open at any one time and close them by means of suitable agreements, one after the other, step by step, by order of importance. One must never try to advance simultaneously on a large number of fronts in turmoil. If necessary, one signs an armistice on one point, one continues the advance and then one returns further on to the previous issue and renegotiates what has been agreed. One cannot overstress the need for patience, flexibility, tenacity and, above all, honesty in order to achieve progress in these processes.

But, in spite of all these difficulties, turnaround projects provide an enormous opportunity for learning to those who take part in them, offer the possibility of changing many things in a short period of time and, if they are done well, the results can be seen immediately, and this tends to produce satisfaction. There is also the ethical factor we have mentioned of preventing the destruction of assets accumulated by society and protecting jobs. We have also said that if it is successful, it is a job that commands a very good remuneration. Thus, in conclusion, those who are faced with a problem of corporate decline and consider they have the skills we have enumerated have the opportunity to enjoy a difficult and rewarding task by acting quickly against the process of decay and its causes.

Bibliography

Bower, J (1986) *When Markets Quake*, Harvard Business School Press, Boston, Mass.

Carlzon, J (1987) *Moments of Truth*, Harper & Row, New York.

Chandler, A D Jr (1990) *Scale and Scope*, The Belknap Press of Harvard University Press, Cambridge, Mass.

Clutterbuck, D (ed) (1985) *New Patterns of Work*, Gower, Aldershot, Hants.

Cusumano, M (1985) *The Japanese Automobile Industry*, Harvard University Press, Cambridge, Mass.

Davis, M (1987) *Turnaround*, Contemporary Books, Chicago, Ill.

Gabarro, J J (1987) *The Dynamics of Taking Charge*, Harvard Business School Press, Boston, Mass.

Harvey-Jones, J (1988) *Making It Happen*, Collins, London.

Hasegawa, F (1988) *Built by Japan*, John Wiley, New York.

Hasegawa, K (1986) *Japanese Style Management*, Kodansha International, Tokyo.

Kanter, E M (1983) *The Change Masters*, Simon & Schuster, New York.

Kanter, E M (1989) *When Giants Learn to Dance*, Simon & Schuster, New York.

Kester, W C (1991) *Japanese Takeovers*, Harvard Business School Press, Boston, Mass.

Kotter, J (1990) *A Force for Change*, The Free Press, New York.

Kuba, Y (1989) *Master Manufacturing Technology*, MD Publications, Tokyo.

McCormack, M H (1984) *What They Don't Teach You at Harvard Business School*, Bantam Books, New York.

Miyazaki, I (1990) *The Japanese Economy*, The Simul Press, Tokyo.

Okimoto, D I (1989) *Between MITI and the Market*, Stanford University Press, Stanford, Calif.

Pinchot, H (1985) *Intrapreneurship*, Harper & Row, New York.

Potts, M and Behr, P (1987) *The Leading Edge*, McGraw-Hill, New York.

Pregel, Suñol, and Nueno, (1989 and 1990) *Instrumentos financieros al servicio de la empresa*, Ediciones Deusto, Bilbao.

Preston, R (1991) *American Steel*, Prentice-Hall, New York.

Quinn Mills, D (1985) *The New Competitors*, John Wiley, New York.

Quinn Mills, D (1991) *Rebirth of the Corporation*, John Wiley, New York.

Sakai, K and Sekiyama, H (1989) *Bunsha*, Intergrace Japan, Tokyo.

Shook, R L (1988) *Honda*, Prentice-Hall, New York.

Shook, R L (1990) *Turnaround*, Prentice-Hall, New York.

Skinner, W (1978) *Manufacturing: in the Corporate Strategy*, John Wiley, New York.

Skinner, W (1985) *Manufacturing The Formidable Competitive Weapon*, John Wiley, New York.

Skinner, W (1986) 'The Focused Factory', *The Harvard Business Review*, July/August.

Index